DATE DUE

MY 2 6 '08			

DEMCO 38-296

FINANCIAL SECTOR OF THE AMERICAN ECONOMY

edited by

STUART BRUCHEY
UNIVERSITY OF MAINE

A GARLAND SERIES

UNITED STATES TRADE RELATIONS WITH THE NEWLY INDUSTRIALIZING COUNTRIES IN THE PACIFIC BASIN

WON KWANG PAIK

GARLAND PUBLISHING, INC.
NEW YORK & LONDON / 1997

ing-in-Publication Data

Paik, Won Kwang, 1960–
     United States trade relations with the newly industrializing
countries of the Pacific basin / Won Kwang Paik.
          p.   cm. — (Financial sector of the American economy)
     Revision of the author's thesis (Ph. D.)—Michigan State
University, 1989.
     Includes bibliographical references and index.
     ISBN 0-8153-2597-5 (alk. paper)
     1. United States—Foreign economic relations—Pacific Area.
2. Pacific Area—Foreign economic relations—United States.
I. Title. II. Series.
HF1456.5.P3P35 1997
382'.0973099—dc21   96-48393

Printed on acid-free, 250-year-life paper
Manufactured in the United States of America

For my family

Contents

List of Tables and Figures

Preface

With the emergence of "new Protectionism" and the resurrection of international political economy as a legitimate field of international relations, international trade and trade relations have, once again, become the focal points of political science inquiries. Given its varied intellectual attractions, the central theme of international trade remains constant: What are the causes of trade relations? Specifically, what factors determine a flow of commodities from country A to country B? There are basically three major types of answers to this question.

The first type, the neo-classical explanation, is a traditional economic argument that the amounts and type of commodities that are traded are not determined by any one individual or any single enterprise. Rather, exchanges are determined by the advantages and disadvantages which are naturally endowed to a particular producer. If a particular person, business firm, or country has a naturally endowed advantage in producing a particular commodity, then that commodity will be exported to another place with a lesser amount of the endowed factor.

The second type, the neo-Marxist explanation, claims that exchanges of commodities are not naturally determined, instead they are structurally distorted. Because of the dialectical nature of the international capitalist system, trade relations are bounded by a nation's status in a system as either an undeveloped or a developed economy. For an undeveloped nation, the nature and types of trade relations will be conditioned and defined by a developed trading partner. In short, trade decisions are made by developed nations and are determined by the conditions surrounding the international system.

The third type, the statist explanation, presupposed the self-interest of nation-states. Political interests, or more broadly speaking national interests, dictate the characteristics of trade relations between countries.

What is to be gained or relinquished in trading or not trading with other countries.

Would trade serve national interests? Would it enhance national power through the elevation of national wealth? Based on such self interested calculations, a nation will pursue trade policies to fulfill its politicized interests. If an exchange of particular commodities is within the domain of perceived national interests, then trade will be allowed. If not, the exchange will simply be interrupted.

This study seeks to test empirically the three competing explanations of international trade with reference to a specific situation: an increased import penetration from the Pacific Basin Newly Industrializing Countries (NICs) into the United States in the 1970's and 80's. The main purpose of the present study is to: First, develop and test the models of international trade relations, specifically between the United States and the Pacific Basin NICs (Singapore, South Korea, Hong Kong, and Taiwan); Second, to evaluate the explanatory power of these models and re-evaluate the soundness of each theoretical perspective; and Third, to provide policy implications to the United States and the Pacific Basin NICs in their trade relations.

The analyses of the present study show that the neo-classical explanation, which focuses on comparative advantage as expressed in endowed production factors, has the highest explanatory power among the individual models. More importantly, the analyses also show that each of the Pacific Basin NICs is profoundly different from one another. Each NIC has a distinct set of determinants for its success in penetrating the U.S. markets. Although dependent, Hong Kong and Taiwan are somewhat more interdependent, Taiwan and South Korea share similar historical and political backgrounds, and Singapore and South Korea exhibit more active governmental interventions.

Mt. Pleasant, Michigan
Won K. Paik

List of Acronyms

AC	Autocorrelation
ACF	Autocorrelation Function
AR-1	First Order Autoregressive Process
AR-K	Kth Order Autoregressive Process
ASEAN	Association of South-Eastern Asian Nations
CA	Comparative Advantage
CF	Domestic Capital Formation
DEP	Dependency
EGLS	Estimated Generalized Least Squares
ER	United States Dollar Exchange Rate
GE	Government Expenditure
GNP	United States Gross Nation Product Growth Rate
HK	Hong Kong
INT	Interdependence
KOR	Republic of Korea
MER	Mercantilist
NIC	Newly Industrializing Country
OLS	Ordinary Least Squares
PACF	Partial Autocorrelation Function
SIG	Singapore
SITC	Standard International Trade Classification
TAW	Taiwan
TD	Trade Dispute
TSUSA	Tariff Schedules of the United States Annotated
UEP	United States Unemployment Rate
USITC	United States International Trade Commission
USTA	United States Total Aid

United States Trade Relations with the Newly Industrializing Countries in the Pacific Basin

I

The Study of International Trade Relations

INTRODUCTION

For many years, international trade has been an essential part of international relations. Traditionally, economists rather than political scientists have paid the most attention to international trade and national policies. Recently, however, with the emergence of "new Protectionism" and the resurrection of international political economy as a legitimate field of international relations, international trade and trade relations have become the focal points of political science inquiries. Given its varied intellectual attractions, the central theme of international trade remains constant: What are the causes of trade relations? Specifically, what factors determine a flow of commodities from country A to country B?

There are basically three major types of answers to this question. The first type is a neoclassical economic explanation which originates in the writings of Adam Smith and David Ricardo. In this explanation, the amounts and types of commodities that are traded are not determined by any single individual or enterprise. Rather, exchanges are determined by the advantages and disadvantages which are naturally endowed to a particular producer. If a particular person, business firm, or country has a naturally endowed advantage in producing a particular commodity, then that commodity will be exported to another place with a less amount of the endowed factor.

The second type of explanation stems loosely from the writing of Karl Marx. Exchanges of commodities are not naturally determined. Rather, they are structurally distorted. Because of the dialectical nature of the international system, trade relations are bound by a nation's status in the system as either an undeveloped or a developed economy. For an

3

undeveloped nation, the nature and types of trade relations will be conditioned and defined by a developing trading partner. In short, trade decisions are made by developed nations and are determined by the conditions surrounding the international capitalist system.

The third type is a political explanation which presupposes the self-interest of nation-states. Political interests, or more broadly speaking national interests, dictate the characteristics of trade relations between countries. What is to be gained or relinquished in trading or not trading with other countries? Would trade serves the national interests? Would it enhance national power through the elevation of national wealth? Based on such self-interested calculations, a nation will pursue trade policies to fulfill its politicized interests. If an exchange of particular commodities is within the domain of perceived national interests, then trade will be allowed. If not, the exchange will simply be interrupted.

Although many attempts have been made to expand our knowledge of international trade, empirical analyses of these explanations, especially for the events of the recent decades, are very sparse and inadequately carried out. The overwhelming tendency is to treat the phenomenon of international trade from a single, nomological dimension. Economic analyses, such as those of Bhagwati, Leamer, and Helpman and Krugman seek to explain international trade in terms of indifference curves, demand functions, and price elasticities.[1] At the same time, the political analyses of Goldstein, Odell, and Cline investigate the institutions of protection, the outcomes of trade conflicts, and the domestic causes of protectionism.[2]

The divergence between economic and political analysis is obvious and understandable. However, this study seeks to recognize the saliency of both economic and political factors in international trade. Increasingly, trade relations are becoming political events and trade decisions are politically determined which coincide with the perceived increase in trade frictions and a fear of trade wars.

In an effort to lessen the gap between two disjointed disciplines, this study seeks to test empirically the three general explanations of international trade with reference to a specific situation: an increased import penetration from the Newly Industrializing Countries (NICs) of the Pacific Basin into the United States in the 1970s and 80s. The main objective of the present study is to:

(1) develop and test the hypotheses of international trade relations, especially between the United States and the Pacific Basin NICs;

(2) evaluate the explanatory power identified in the hypotheses;

(3) Reevaluate the soundness of each theoretical perspective; and

(4) examine the plausibility of a new theory of international trade, based on the findings of the study.

Given these intentions, the present study examines interdependence, dependency, and mercantilist theories of trade relations. Additionally, the study seeks to investigate these theories from the several levels of analysis. Import penetrations from the NICs into the United States will be investigated using the national total and the totals from the processing levels of commodities. The six "levels of processing of exports" developed by Firebaugh and Bullock will be followed for clustering various commodities. This categorization of exports is based on the amount of technology and capital required to process commodities for exports. Exports are classified into three levels of primary products and three levels of manufactured goods.[3] Empirical tests will be performed at the aggregated regional level, the aggregated national level, and the clusters of commodities level. In so doing, I am seeking not only to evaluate each theory's relevance at the national (macro) level, but also to determine its explanatory power at the commodity (micro) level of analysis.

The study investigates trade relations between the Pacific Basin NICs, (i.e., Singapore, South Korea, Hong Kong, and Taiwan) and the United States. The Pacific Basin NICs were chosen for several reasons. First of all, the Pacific Basin is an economically dynamic region. Linder tells us that the Pacific Basin NICs "...spectacular growth shows greater resilience than that of the South European and Latin American NICs."[4] Moreover, Cline maintains that, among the developing countries, South Korea, Hong Kong, Taiwan, and Singapore showed the most dramatic growth in shares in the market for manufactured imports in industrial countries. Clearly, the Pacific Basin NICs (sometimes called the Gang of Four or the Four Little Japans) are the most rapidly developing and the most actively trading economies among developing countries.[5]

Secondly, the Pacific Basin is a politically important region. It has an undeniable strategic importance. Sneider claims that "the region is dependent for its security on United States military power....The United States, in turn, must constantly reinforce the credibility of its commitments and maintain a consistent involvement."[6] Indeed, the United States has a fundamental commitment to the Pacific Basin to prevent hostile powers such as the former Soviet Union and North Korea from expanding their control over the region and to maintain sufficient power to thwart any direct or indirect threat.

Thirdly, although the Pacific Basin NICs share many common characteristics, there are also considerable differences among them. For instance, each NIC has a distinct historical origin of statehood. Harris affirms that although Hong Kong lacks a state in the development sense, the government (of Hong Kong) does more than it acknowledges, more than what officials call 'sitting on our hands.'[7] Each stems from history, culture, and tradition. Each pursues different economic policies toward development. And currently, each NIC faces profoundly different domestic and international demands and conditions.

In short, the Pacific Basin offers an interesting empirical referent for international trade study. It is economically vigorous, politically important, and sufficiently distinct in many ways. Analyzing import penetrations by the Pacific Basin NICs requires the consideration of the similarities and the dissimilarities within the region. It offers enough variation to be meaningful, but not so much that comparisons become extremely complicated and data collection difficult.

THEORETICAL REVIEW

In the field of international political economy, there are three major theoretical perspectives concerned with trade relations. They are, Interdependence (Liberalism), Dependency (Marxism), and Mercantilism (Realism). At the risk of oversimplification, I will summarize the main points of each perspective in an attempt to isolate the consistent and prevalent causes of import penetration.

Interdependence Theory

The term "interdependence" was introduced in the eighteenth century by the physiocrats in France and by bourgeois critics of governmental economic policy in Great Britain. They were critical of self-interested, mercantilist policies pursued by their governments and introduced the term as an ideal to be achieved in a new liberal political and economic order.

Interdependence theory maintains that an open trading system characterized by the free flow of goods with minimum political intervention (i.e., less protectionism) produces the most efficient economic system. Based on the liberal view of human nature, interdependence theory assumes that individuals are the center of creative and productive activity and that the state is an inefficient and restrictive body which curtails economic activity. Interdependence theory argues that the state should not regulate economic activity because state regulations interrupt economic growth, whereas a free market (trade) leads to innovation and growth through competition. Such a system of free trade, in turn, will produce maximum economic welfare for the trading nations and for the world as a whole.

Gilpin notes that

> Liberals argue...the state should not interfere with economic transactions across national boundaries. Through free exchange of commodities, removal of restrictions on the flow of investment, and an international division of labor, everyone will benefit in the long run as a result of a more efficient utilization of the world's scarce resources.[8]

Likewise, Walleri affirms that "in its original formulation, the liberal world view stressed the notions of laissez-faire capitalism, the rights of property, limited government, and Social Darwinism. Assuming perfect competition, the market would produce maximum economic growth, development, and general welfare."[9]

Waltz describes the main argument of interdependence theory as follows:

> Do Michigan and Florida gain by trading freely the automobiles of the one for the oranges of the other? Or would Michigan be richer growing its own oranges under glass, instead of importing the produce of "foreign" labor? The answer is obvious.... Each side gains from trade, whether between individuals, corporations, localities, or nations. Otherwise, no trade would take place.[10]

In a similar vein, Morse states that "the system of individual liberty in a free market would enable society as a whole to achieve a higher level of material benefit than would be feasible under mercantilism."[11] Strange makes a stronger assertion that "the main tenet of liberal economics regarding international trade is that the less governments intervene to obstruct the flow of trade, the better."[12] Strange adds that as liberal policies toward foreign competition are adopted, national welfare and global welfare will be better served.[13]

Based on the assumption that "*an invisible hand*" seems to be working in the area of economic policy as well as in the marketplace, interdependence theory promotes the doctrine of free trade. It argues that free trade allows the most effective allocation of resources in the production of goods and services, thus producing maximum national and global welfare. Walleri concludes that "combined with unrestricted movement of capital, free trade would maximize world production through optimal efficiency in resource allocation. Any maldistribution resulting from global economic transaction, conducted according to liberal principles, is considered to be only minor."[14]

Essentially, interdependence theory stems from the classical economic writings of Adam Smith and David Ricardo. In his *Wealth of Nations*, Adam Smith had ridiculed the fear of trade by comparing nations to households. Smith argued that since every household finds it worthwhile to produce only some of its needs and to buy others from his neighboring producers, the same logic should apply to nations:

> It is the maxim of every prudent master of a family, never to attempt to make at home what it will cost him more to make than to buy. The tailor does not attempt to make his own shoes, but buys them from the shoemaker....What is prudence in the conduct of every private family, can scarce be folly in that of a great kingdom. If a foreign country can supply us with a commodity cheaper than we ourselves can make it, better buy it of them with some part of the produce of our own industry, employed in a way in which we have some advantage.[15]

Following Adam Smith's liberal economic view, David Ricardo formulated the doctrine of comparative cost to explain international trade. The value of goods is determined in each country by the amount of labor required to produce them, but this need not be the same in different countries. Labor may be more productive in one country than in another, so that different amounts of labor are required to produce given goods.[16]

Ricardo showed that the gains from trade accrue to both sides even when a country has no absolute advantage whatsoever. As long as the price ratio differs at all between countries in the absence of trade, every country will have a comparative advantage, an ability to produce some goods at lower relative cost disadvantage than other goods. The country should export these goods in exchange for some of the others.

The notion of comparative advantage, as argued by David Ricardo, is formally presented as the Heckscher-Ohlin model in the international trade literature. In short, the model states that a country's trading relations with the rest of the world depend on its endowments of productive factors, identified as land, labor and capital.

Kindleberger and Lindert summarize the Heckscher-Ohlin explanation of trade patterns as follows:

> ...different goods require different factor production, and different countries have different relative factor endowments; therefore countries will tend to have comparative advantages in producing the goods that use their more abundant factors more intensively; for this reason each country will end up exporting its abundant factor good in exchange for imported goods that use its scarce factor more intensively.[17]

More analytically, Leamer outlines the two major assumptions of the comparative advantage model: (1) there are factors of production that are immobile between countries, and (2) these factors are used in different combinations to produce different goods.[18]

Accordingly, the model posits that a country will possess a comparative advantage in good *X* if the country is relatively well endowed with factors that are used intensively in the production of *X*. This law of comparative advantage views trade as essentially a way for countries to benefit from their differences. Because countries differ in climate, culture, skills, resources and so on, each country will have a comparative advantage in producing goods for which its particular character suits it. Consequently, the comparative advantage model tells us that a country will export the commodity that uses intensively its relative abundant factor. Countries with relatively large labor forces have a comparative advantage in the commodity that exhibits relatively large scale economies.[19]

The principle of comparative advantage, Krugman maintains, "...leads one to expect to see trade dominated by exchanges that reflect the particular strengths of economies -- for instance, exports of manufactures by advanced countries and exports of raw materials by underdeveloped countries."[20] In a similar vein, Brander contends that trade relations and patterns are determined by comparative advantage, and free markets are the best way of exploiting comparative advantage.[21] As such, interdependence theory explains that international trade relations are stimulated by comparative advantages and that the system of free trade creates maximum economic growth and benefit.

Dependency Theory

Dependency theory argues that the world trading system is characterized by an unequal exchange of goods between developed and undeveloped countries. In the Marxist tradition, dependency theory focuses on the modes of production. Each mode of production defines a pair of opposed classes, a class of producers (proletariat) and a non-producing class (bourgeoisie) that exploits them. Marx posits that the modes of production determine the structure of society and state. More precisely, Marx argues that society is shaped by the dominant mode of production, and the relationship inherent in that mode will determine the role of the state. Marx articulates that capitalism is a stage in the continuous progression of human economic organization which is preceded by communalism and feudalism and will eventually be replaced with communism.

Emerging from these basic notions, dependency theory articulates that a capitalist world economy (liberal or otherwise) will continue to breed underdevelopment in undeveloped countries.[22]

In its original formulation, dependency theory claims that the economic and political institutions in underdeveloped countries are the product of the historical development of the world capitalist system. This system is delineated by the economic and political domination of developed countries over undeveloped countries. The main argument of the dependency theory is that:

> The 'metropolis' or 'core' exploits the 'satellites' or 'peripheral' by direct extraction of profit or tribute, by 'unequal' exchange or through monopolistic control over trade. Underdevelopment is not a state of original backwardness, but is the result of the imposition of a particular pattern of specialization and exploitation in the periphery.[23]

Similarly, Gilpin affirms that

> The argument of dependencia [*dependency*] thesis is that the economic dependence of the underdeveloped

periphery upon the developed core is responsible for the impoverishment of the former. Development and underdevelopment are simultaneous processes: the developed countries have progressed and have grown rich through exploiting the poor and making them poorer. Lacking true autonomy and being economically dependent upon the developed countries, the underdeveloped countries have suffered because the developed have a veto over their development.[24]

Dos Santos defines dependence as a situation in which the economy of certain countries is conditioned by the development and expansion of another economy to which the former is subjected.[25] A dependent relation exists when some countries (the dominant, core ones) can expand and can be self-sustaining, while other countries (the dependent, peripheral ones) can do this only as a reflection of that expansion.

Dos Santos says historic forms of dependence are conditioned by: (1) the basic form of the capitalist world economy which has its own law of development; (2) the type of economic relations dominant in the capitalist center and the warp in which the latter expand outward; and (3) the type of economic relations existing inside the peripheral countries which are incorporated into the situation of dependence within the network of international economic relations generated by capitalist expansion.[26]

Frank contends that "the economic, political, social, and cultural institutions and relations we now observe there (in underdeveloped countries) are the products of the historical development of the capitalist system no less than are the seemingly more modern or capitalist features of the national metropolis of these underdeveloped countries."[27] Moreover, Frank argues that, in the 'metropolis-satellite' structure, each of the satellites serves as an instrument to extract capital or economic surplus out of its own satellite and to channel part of this surplus to the world metropolis. In addition, each metropolis serves to impose and maintain the monopolistic structure and exploitative relationship of this system as long as it serves the interests of the metropolis which take advantage of this structure to promote their own development and enrichment of their ruling classes.[28]

The dependent relationship is characterized by the domination of big capital in the hegemonic centers and its expansion abroad through investment in the production of raw materials and agricultural products for consumption in the hegemonic center. A productive structure in the dependent countries is conditioned by the export of these products. And as such, the production is determined by demand from the hegemonic center and the internal productive structure is characterized by rigid specialization and monoculture in the entire region. In this vein, DosSantos concludes,

> ...(a dependent economic system) reproduces a productive system whose development is limited by those world relations which necessarily lead to the development of only certain economic sectors, to trade under unequal condition, to domestic competition with international capital under unequal conditions to the imposition of relations of super-exploitation of the domestic labor force with a view to dividing the economic surplus thus generated between internal external forces of domination.[29]

Ultimately, dependency theory maintains that such relationships facilitate more dependent economies and backwardness in the peripheral countries. The development of dependent capitalism benefits very narrow sectors, encounters unyielding domestic obstacles to its continued economic growth (with respect to both internal and foreign markets), and leads to the progressive accumulation of balance of payment deficits, which in turn generate more dependence and more superexploitation.

Dependent development, as the modified version of dependency theory, introduces the concept of the semi-periphery. The concept of semi-periphery originates from Wallerstein. In his world system analysis, Wallerstein equates capitalism and world economy: "Capitalism and a world economy (that is, a single division of labor but multiple polities) are obverse sides of the same coin."[30] Although Wallerstein undertakes a holistic approach (few are likely to disagree), I will limit the scope of this study to dependency theory since Wallerstein's arguments have a great deal in common with those of dependency. This version views the international trading system as an exploitative system consisting of the core, semi-periphery, and periphery. Still, in such an exploitative trading system, power and decision are lodged in the urban financial and industrial cores and the lack of true autonomy and economic dependence are inevitable for the peripheries and the semi-peripheries. More importantly, the strategy of capital accumulation for a dependent state is conditioned by its relation to the international economy.

Although the modified version of dependency theory recognizes the possibility of development conjoined with dependence, there are many distortions associated with dependent development. Examining the distortions generated by the "tripod" alliance of multinational, state, and local capital in Brazil, Evans concludes that "...(dependent development) excludes most of the national bourgeoisie from political participation just as it excludes the mass of the population."[31] Similarly, Cardoso argues that dependent development will lead to (1) more dependent economies, as shown by increased foreign indebtedness, (2) income inequalities as the gap between rich and poor grows wider, and (3) authoritarian regimes since states are "captured" by foreign capital which seeks controlled climates for investment.[32]

Modified dependency theory, as an economic explanation, argues that economic factors motivated by capitalist interests are the major cause of dependent relationships and rejects the significance of nation-state as an independent actor. Evans claims that the collaboration within the "tripod" alliance is based on a common respect for the logic of profitability.[33]

Obviously, dependency theory sees the world trading system not as a collection of individual nation states working together to foster mutual benefits, but as a structured capitalist system operating under the principles of unequal exchange of goods and benefits. Spero explains that

> Trade between North and South is a process of unequal exchange, as control of the international market by developed capitalist countries leads to a declining price for the raw materials produced by the South and a rising price for industrial products produced by the North. Thus the terms of trade of the international market are structured against the South. In addition, international trade encourages the South to concentrate on backward forms of production which prevent development.[34]

Emphasizing "monopolistic" structures and "exploitative" relationships, dependency theory argues that the trade relations between the core and the peripheries are devised to serve the economic interests of the core countries. The major implication of dependency theory is that a dependent economy is conditioned and controlled by the development and expansion of core economies. In other words, the economic conditions and circumstances of core nations will dominate trade relations. Changes in the core economic conditions, as seen by improved or worsened general economic conditions, will be directly related to the import performance of developing countries. Moreover, as the consequences of dependent relationships, a dependent state will be associated with the development of only certain economic sectors, limited export commodities, unequal trade conditions, increased balance-of-payment deficits, and foreign indebtedness.

Mercantilism

In contrast to interdependence and dependency theory, mercantilism emphasizes the primacy of politics over economic factors. Gilpin boldly states that "international economic relations are in reality political relations."[35] Historically, mercantilism was a rationale for the policies of the dynamic ruling groups who formed the modern European nation-states. Morse tells us that mercantilism

> ...justified the elimination of internal tariffs and taxes that provided revenues for lesser feudal groups who were viewed as potential rivals. The dynamic rulers were interested in creating effective customs' unions within their newly formed states as a means of enhancing their own power and building up unified economic and political systems.[36]

Although mercantilism as an economic doctrine does not have a coherent body of literature since early mercantilist writers were not interested in constructing theoretical explanations. Mercantilists were interested in attaining specific political and economic goals that would elevate the state's power and wealth. The principal contention is that the nation state and the interplay of national interest (as distinct from corporate interest) are the primary determinants of the world economy.

Gilpin defines mercantilism as "the attempt of government to manipulate economic arrangements in order to maximize its own interest, whether or not this is at the expense of others."[37] These interests may be related to domestic concerns (i.e., full employment, price stability) or to foreign policy (i.e., security, interdependence). Basically, according to mercantilism, each nation will pursue economic policies that reflect domestic economic needs and external political ambitions without much concern for the effects of these policies on other countries or on the international economic system as a whole.

Specifically, mercantilism stresses the importance of maximizing power, which is identified with wealth. According to Morse, this mercantilist desire is based on the assumptions that

> (1) wealth is an absolutely essential means to power, whether for security or for aggression;
> (2) power is essential or valuable as a means to the acquisition or retention of wealth;
> (3) wealth and power are each proper ultimate ends of national policy; and
> (4) there is long-run harmony between these ends, although in particular circumstances it may be necessary for a time to make economic sacrifices in the interest of military security and therefore also of long-term prosperity.[38]

Likewise, Gilpin asserts that mercantilism means the reciprocal and dynamic interaction in international relations of the pursuit of wealth and pursuit of power.[39] In the short run, the distributions of power and the nature of the political system are major determinants of the framework within which wealth is produced and distributed. In the long run, however, shifts in economic efficiency and in the location of economic activity tend to undermine and transform the existing political system. Walleri notes that mercantilism emphasizes the role of the state in promoting economic growth and development rather than emphasizing the role of the self-regulating market.[40] In particular, the state should eliminate internal barriers to trade, subsidize the creation of infrastructures, and promote home industry and the export of manufactures.

Analyzing the economic rationale of mercantilism, Hirschman elaborates the possible use of foreign trade as an instrument of national power policy.[41] Krasner , in his discussion of "state-power" theory and its relationship with the structure of international trade, contends that trade relations can only be understood within the context of the power and interests of states. In their quest for wealth, mercantilists assume that a nation can increase its wealth only by decreasing the wealth of other nations.[42] As such, Hirschman constructs a syllogism to demonstrate the connection established by the mercantilists between wealth and national power:

> *Major premise*: An increase of wealth of any country is an
> increase of its absolute power, and vice versa.
> *Minor premise*: An increase of wealth of any country, if
> brought about by foreign trade, is necessarily a loss of wealth
> for other countries.
> *Conclusion*: An increase of wealth through foreign trade leads
> to an increase of power relative to that of other countries--
> precisely the political aim of mercantilist policy.[43]

Hirschman concludes that trade policies are molded by the interests of power policy and are implemented to enhance the state's power position against other states. By viewing trade as the means of accumulating wealth which is convertible to power, mercantilism focuses on the attempt of governments to manipulate economic arrangements in order to maximize their own interest. Accordingly, the state plays a central role in overseeing all facets of trade, with the ultimate purpose of building the power of the state.[44]

Economic doctrines of mercantilism are closely related to more traditional notions of realism. Broadly, mercantilism can be viewed as a subset of the realist's paradigm, encouraging economic nationalism and a strong central government while sharing fundamental assumptions. Essentially, three assumptions are integral to the realist vision: (1) states as coherent units are the dominant actors in world politics; (2) force is a useful and effective instrument of policy; and (3) there is a hierarchy of issues in world politics, headed by questions of military security.[45]

Realists depict a world in which politics is continually characterized by active or potential conflict among states, with the use of force possible at any time. Each state attempts to defend its territory and interest from real or perceived threats. In such a system, political integration is minimized and lasts only as long as it serves the interests of particular states. Subsequently, according to Keohane and Nye, "...(realism) insists that national security is the primary national goal and that in international politics security threats are permanent."[46]

The central theme of mercantilism is that although the economic and technical substructure partially determines and interacts with the political superstructure, political values and security interests are crucial determinants of international economic relations, including trade relations. In short, politics determines the framework of economic activity and channels it in directions which tend to serve the political objectives of dominant political groups and organizations. Furthermore, Keohane and Nye claim that although international economic activity appears to be nonpolitical, it does not mean that political power is unimportant. Indeed the effect of politics may be indirect; it may determine the relationship within which day-to-day processes take place.[47] Gilpin unequivocally points out that "the primary actors in the international system are nation-states in pursuit of what they define as their national-interest."[48]

The mercantilist perspective implies that the structure of international trade is determined by the interests and power of states acting to maximize national goals. Theoretically, the state is viewed to be an autonomous actor and the objectives sought by the state are regarded as the national interests. With respect to trade relations, the state must appraise two distinct sets of national interests: the national security interest and the mercantilistic economic interest.

On the one hand, the state must examine its national security objectives in dealing with trade questions. For trade to be possible, there must be a convergence of the national security objectives. That is, two states must share some common ideas, some common world view or ideological commitment. This condition explains the inherent difficulty associated with (or the lack of) East-West trade relations. Clearly, it is not an economic problem. Rather a divergence in the national security interests held by the United States and the former Soviet Union which explains the minimum level of trade relations. In any event, the state must consider its mercantilistic economic objectives. What economic arrangements can it manipulate to maximize its interest? Which trade policy will bring forth the greatest benefit? The state, with the ultimate aim of elevating its wealth, will follow the trade policy which will reflect its domestic economic needs, i.e., full employment, sustained growth rate, price stability, etc.

WHAT IS TO BE DONE?

This survey of the literature that attempts to explain international trade relations has demonstrated the multifaceted nature of import penetration. Interdependence theory views import penetration simply as an economic phenomenon driven by the forces of comparative advantages. The theory implies that micro-economic factors, especially those naturally endowed production and labor factors have a significant cause of the NICs' import penetration into the United States. Dependency theory argues that the macro economic conditions and the circumstances surrounding the international capitalist system will determine trade relations. In other words, the external demands and conditions which surround the NICs will determine their rate of penetration into the U.S. market. Mercantilist theory considers import penetration as a result of shrewd political calculations masterminded by the "Prince-like" political actors. Convergence of the national security interest with the U.S. coupled with the mercantilistic export policies of the Pacific Basin NICs will the key determinants in explaining the NICs' import penetration into the United States.

At this point, it seems reasonable to provide an overview of the present study in order to provide the readers some guidelines to navigate through the study's research direction.

First, the linkages between the theoretical perspectives and their hypotheses will be constructed inasmuch as the theories permit. For instance, interdependence theory is very precise in terms of its theoretical rigor, making a clear connection between the processing (or the commodity) level and import penetration. Dependency and especially mercantilist theory, on the hand, are considerably less precise, only vaguely suggesting that the relationship at the processing (or the commodity) level of import penetration--perhaps--exists.

Second, key concepts will be defined to approximate their respective theoretical constructs. The indicators will be constructed based on the available data and the appropriate means of data computation will be employed. Third, the data will be checked for the various methodological concerns, particularly for trends and autocorrelations. Lastly, the interpretations of the results and implications (both theoretical and policy-oriented) will be presented and elaborated. It is clear that the present study only deals with U.S. import penetration from the Newly Industrializing Countries of the Pacific Basin within a specific time period, and its findings are by no means universal nor final. They may or may not be generalized to other places or time periods.

NOTES

1. Jagdish Bhagwati, ed., *Import Competition and Response* (Chicago: University of Chicago Press, 1982); Edward E. Leamer, *Sources of International Comparative Advantage: Evidence and Theory* (Cambridge, MA: MIT Press, 1984); Elhanan Helpman, "International Trade in the Presence of Product Differentiation, Economies of Scale and Monopolistic Competition: A Chamberlin-Heckscher-Ohlin Approach," *Journal of International Economics* 11 (September 1981): 305-340; and Paul R. Krugman, "Introduction: New Thinking About Trade Policy," in *Strategic Trade Policy and New International Economics, ed.* Krugman (Cambridge, MA: MIT Press, 1986).

2. Judith Goldstein, "The Political Economy of Trade," *American Political Science Review* 80 (1986):161-184; John S. Odell, "The Outcomes of International Trade Conflicts: The US and South Korea, 1960-1980," *International Studies Quarterly* 29 (1985): 263-286; and William R. Cline, *Exports of Manufactured From Developing Countries* (Washington, D.C.: Brookings Institute, 1984).

3. Glenn Firebaugh and Bradley P. Bullock, "Level of Processing of Exports: Estimates for Developing Nations," *International Studies Quarterly* 30 (1986): 333-350.

4. Stefan B. Linder, *The Pacific Century: Economic and Political Consequences of Asian Pacific Dynamism* (Stanford: Stanford University Press, 1986), p. 4.

5. See Cline, p. 9.

6. Richard Sneider, "United States Security Interest," in *The Pacific Basin: New Challenges for the United States*, ed. James Morley (New York: Academy of Political Science, 1986), p. 83.

7. Niegel Harris, *The End of the Third World: Newly Industrializing Countries and the Decline of an Ideology* (New York: Penguin Books, 1986), p. 59.

8. Robert Gilpin, "The Nature of Political Economy," in *International Politics, ed.* Robert Art and Robert Jervis (Boston: Little Brown and Company, 1985), p. 279.

9. Dan R. Walleri, "The Political Economy Literature of North-South Relations," *International Studies Quarterly* 22 (1978): 592-593.

10. Kenneth Waltz, *Man, the State, and War: A Theoretical Analysis* (New York: Columbia University Press, 1954), p. 98-99.

11. Edward L. Morse, "Interdependence in World Affairs," in *World*

Politics, ed. James Rosneau (New York: Free Press, 1976), p. 661.

12. Susan Strange, "Protectionism and World Politics," *International Organization* 39 (1985): 233-259.

13. Ibid.

14. Walleri, p. 594.

15. Adam Smith, *An Inquiry into the Nature and Causes of the Wealth of Nations* (Chicago: University of Chicago Press, 1976), p. 424-425.

16. David Ricardo, *The Principles of Political Economy and Taxation.* (London: Dent and Sons, 1973).

17. Charles P. Kindleberger and Peter H. Lindert, *International Economics* (Homewood, IL: Richard Irwin, Inc., 1978), p. 30.

18. Edward E. Leamer, *Sources of International Comparative Advantage: Theory and Evidence,* (Cambridge, MA: MIT Press, 1984), p. xiii.

19. Ibid., p. 47.

20. Krugman, p. 7.

21. James A. Brander, "Rationales for Strategic Trade and Industrial Policy," in *Strategic Trade Policy and New International Economics*, ed. Paul Krugman (Cambridge, MA: MIT Press, 1986).

22. Walleri, p. 589.

23. Anthony Brewer, *Marxist Theories of Imperialism: A Critical Survey* (London: Routledege&Kegan Paul, 1980), p. 17.

24. Robert Gilpin, "Three Models of the Future," in *World Politics and International Economics*, ed. C. Fred Bergsten and Lawrence Krause (Washington D.C.: Brookings Institute, 1975), p. 44.

25. Theotonio Dos Santos, "Historical Perspectives on Political Economy," in *International Politics, ed.* Robert Art and Robert Jervis (Boston: Little Brown and Company, 1985), p. 303.

26. Ibid., p. 304.

27. Andre Gunder Frank,"The Development of Underdevelopment," *Monthly Review* 18 (1966), p. 19.

28. Ibid.

29. Dos Santos, p. 310.

30. Immanuel Wallerstein, *The Capitalist World Economy* (London: Cambridge University Press, 1979), p. 6.

31. Peter Evans, *Dependent Development: The Alliance of Multinational, State and Local Capital in Brazil* (Princeton: Princeton University Press, 1979), p. 50.

32. Fernando H. Cardoso, "Associated-Dependent Development," in

Authoritarian Brazil, ed. Alfred Stephan (New Haven: Yale University Press, 1973).

33. Evans, p. 50.

34. Joan Edelman Spero, *The Politics of International Economic Relations* (New York: St. Martin's Press, 1985), p. 139.

35. Gilpin, "Political Economy," p. 286.

36. Morse, p. 661.

37. Gilpin, "Three Models," p. 45.

38. Morse, p. 661.

39. Gilpin, "Political Economy," p. 289.

40. Walleri, p. 590-591.

41. Albert Hirschman, *National Power and the Structure of Foreign Trade* (Berkeley: University of California Press, 1980).

42. Stefan B. Krasner, "State Power and the Structure of International Trade," *World Politics* 28 (1976): 317-348.

43. Hirschman, p. 4-5.

44. Ibid.

45. Robert Keohane and Joseph Nye, *Power and Interdependence: World Politics in Transition* (Boston: Little Brown, and Company, 1989), p. 23-24.

46. Ibid., p. 6.

47. Keohane and Nye, p. 23-24.

48. Ibid., p. 286.

II

The Determinants of Import Penetration

The previous chapter argued that import penetration is a complex phenomenon, conceptually linked to various causal factors. One might distinguish these causal factors on the basis of their general orientations and the scope of analysis. First, some are primarily economic factors while others are predominantly political. Second, the causal factors have either international (external/macro) or domestic (internal/micro) emphasis. Taken together, causal factors can be categorized into four broad classifications: international economic, domestic economic, international political, and domestic political. This overall categorization will serve as the guidepost in formulating operational hypotheses within each theoretical perspective.

A descriptive analysis of import penetration into the United States by the NICs, at different level of processing indicates that while the general imports of the United States have grown substantially, the NICs' share of U.S. imports has increased at a faster rate. Moreover, the trends in levels of processing show that the NICs' shares for the commodities which require medium processing skills (i.e., Levels 4 and 5 commodities) had the most impressive growth rates, whereas the lower processing goods (i.e., Level 1 and 2 commodities) produced the minimum increases.[1]

THE TREND OF IMPORT PENETRATION

The annual trends of import penetration display several interesting points. In terms of dollar values, the U.S. general imports have increased consistently. As indicated in Table 2.1, the gross value of U.S. general

23

Table 2.1: Annual Total U.S. Imports and Imports from the NICs,
1967 - 1985 (in million $)

YEAR	U.S.	NICs	SIG	KOR	HK	TAW
1967	15339	428	8	61	272	87
1968	33114	1134	29	199	637	270
1969	36052	1549	55	291	815	388
1970	39963	1945	81	370	945	549
1971	45602	2406	136	462	991	817
1972	55555	3515	265	708	1249	1293
1973	69121	4646	459	971	1444	1772
1974	100972	5758	553	1460	1637	2108
1975	96940	5494	534	1442	1573	1946
1976	121793	8544	697	2440	2408	2999
1977	147022	10324	881	2883	2894	3666
1978	172025	13495	1103	3747	3474	5171
1979	206327	15421	1467	4047	4006	5901
1980	240834	17653	1920	4147	4736	6850
1981	261305	20732	2114	5141	5428	8049
1982	243952	22264	2195	5637	5540	8893
1983	258048	27614	2868	7148	6394	11204
1984	325726	36366	3979	9353	8266	14768
1985	345276	39066	4260	10013	8396	16396

Source: U.S. Department of Commerce, *U.S. General Imports: World Area by Commodity Groupings*.

imports has gone up from 15 billion dollars in 1967 to 345 billion in 1985, more than a 20-fold increase. For the NICs, their share of U.S. imports sustained a faster rate of increases than that of U.S. imports as a whole. In fact, during the time period of the study, the NICs' share went up by 91 times; its value grew from less than a half billion to 390 billion dollars. Singapore displayed the highest rate of increases, registering a 533-fold increase, followed by Taiwan (188), Korea (164) and Hong Kong (31). The import penetration from the Pacific Basin NICs is a significant portion of U.S. import and the NICs became increasingly important trade partners for the U.S.

Measured as the percent of U.S. general imports, Figure 2.1 displays the NICs' import penetration between 1967 and 1985. The NICs' share, while controlling for the size of U.S. imports, has risen from 2.8 percent to 11.3 percent. In other words, since 1983, more than 10 percent of everything that we import originates from the "Gang of Four." This is the largest record of U.S. import penetrations shown by any group of NICs, including the Latin American and the South East Asian NICs.

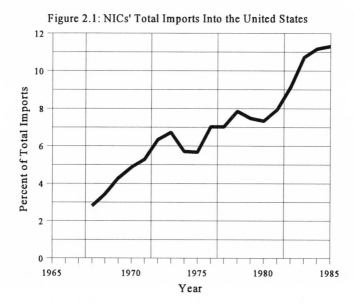

Figure 2.1: NICs' Total Imports Into the United States

Furthermore, with the exceptions of 1974 and 1979, the NICs enjoyed increased import penetrations each year over the previous year's total. The exceptions are probably associated with the global economic hardship caused by the OPEC oil crisis in 1974 and the severe economic recession experienced by the U.S. in 1979.

As indicated by Figure 2.2, Hong Kong began as the largest trading partner among the NICs, only to be overtaken by Taiwan in 1972. Hong Kong and Korea competed for the number two spot during the late 1970s, but Korea emerged as the solid second after 1982. Singapore, meanwhile, continues to be the smallest of the Four, probably because it is the smallest economy among the Pacific Basin NICs.

Figure 2.2: Each NICs' Total Imports into the United States

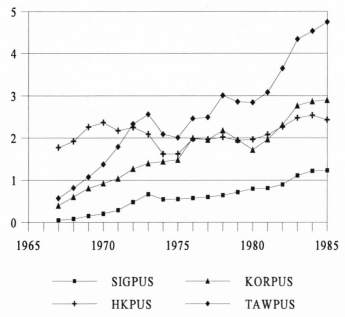

During this time period, Taiwan recorded the most remarkable growth, elevating its U.S. market share from 0.6 percent to about 5 percent.The increases for the other NICs were: Korea, from 0.4 percent to 2.9 percent; Hong Kong, from 1.8 percent to 2.4 percent, and Singapore, from 0.05 percent to 1.2 percent.

Hong Kong, which began as the top exporting NIC, had the lowest rate of growth of import penetration, eventually becoming a distant third among the Four. The data on levels of processing of exports (commodities that belong to the six levels of processing are given in Appendix A) provide some insights as to why.

Figure 2.3: NICs' Imports for the Six Levels of Commodities

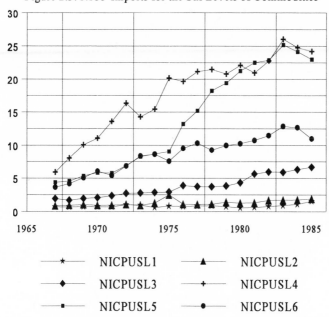

——★——	NICPUSL1	——▲——	NICPUSL2
——◆——	NICPUSL3	——+——	NICPUSL4
——■——	NICPUSL5	——●——	NICPUSL6

At the aggregate NICs level, Figure 2.3 displays that Level 1 and Level 2 commodities, which are agricultural and primary products, experienced the lowest growth rate of import penetration. Level 5 (medium-high processed products) demonstrated the most impressive growth, very closely followed by Level 4, which consist of labor-intensive commodities. Levels 3 and 6 commodities have had only marginal growth rates from the aggregate perspective. In all, the trends in levels of processing signify that much of the NICs' import penetrations can be attributed to commodities with a medium level of processing, such as wearing apparel, footwear, steel, chemicals, plastic materials, and metal products, whereas commodities with a low level of processing, i.e., food products, leather goods, textile fibers, and fertilizers, did not enhance the NICs' trading position against the U.S.

The individual NIC's import penetration with regard to commodity level penetration is displayed in Table 2.2. Reported as percent of each NIC's total import into the U.S., it shows similarities and dissimilarities among the NICs. First, it seems that Singapore is the only NIC exporting any significant amount of agricultural and food-processed products,averaging about 20 percent of its total import. Second, all four NICs rely heavily on Level 4 and 6 commodities for the U.S. market penetration. For instance, about 60 percent of Singapore's import into the U.S. consists of Level 6 or high-tech commodities. Similarly, Level 6 commodities account for 46 percent for Hong Kong 's and 40 percent of Taiwan's import penetration. South Korea, along with Taiwan and Hong Kong, has relied mostly on Level 4 which consist of labor-intensive commodities. Lastly, Table 2.2 shows that all four NICs are less active in penetration of Level 3 commodities, coinciding with Figure 2.3.

Table 2.2: Individual NIC's Import in Commodity
Level As Percent of Total Import

	SIG	KOR	HK	TAW
Level 1	9.4	3.7	1.1	5.8
Level 2	10.9	.4	.3	2.2
Level 3	2.7	4.2	6.6	3.7
Level 4	16.1	53.9	38.6	39.3
Level 5	1.3	7.6	7.2	8.7
Level 6	59.6	30.3	46.2	40.3

To recapitulate, trade data and trends indicate that first, the NICs' overall import penetration show a higher rate of growth than that of U.S. imports as a whole. Second, at the aggregated regional level, the success of the NICs' import penetration can be attributed to the impressive growth in commodities with a medium level of processing, including wearing apparel, footwear, steel, and chemicals and to a lesser degree attributed to high-tech and primary commodities. Third, the bulk of Singapore's import into the U.S. consists of Level 6 commodities; Korea relies mostly on Level 4 and 6; Hong Kong, while dropping to the third spot among the Four, continues to concentrates on Level 4 and 6. Taiwan, which replaced Hong Kong in the top spot, focuses on Level 4, 5, and 6 as its main stake in penetrating the U.S. market.

Although this analysis points out several interesting patterns of the NICs' import penetration, the questions still remain: Why is it the case that the NICs experienced increased import penetrations? Why are there variations in import penetrations at different levels of processing? And why do different NICs have different rates of penetration at different levels? To deal with these questions, causal factors, suggested by the competing theoretical perspectives will be isolated, in order to formulate the operational hypotheses of import penetrations.

THE CAUSES OF IMPORT PENETRATION

Interdependence Hypotheses

The Interdependence perspective assumes that the relations between states are fundamentally harmonious, not conflictual. Simply put, international trade is a positive-sum game; everyone gains, and no one needs to lose, from a proper ordering of trade relations. Interdependence emphasizes the significance of economic interests and actors. For example, business corporations and other economic interests are conceived as the significant actors in shaping the structure of the international trading system.

In this dynamic system, the national interest is best served by generous and cooperative interactions among economic interests--"the pursuit of self-interest in a free, competitive economy achieves the greatest good for the greatest number in international no less than in the national society."[2] As such, interdependence contends that economic conditions, motivated by a free exchange of commodities and international division of labor, will determine the nature and level of trade relations.

As explained by Adam Smith, David Ricardo, and Heckscher-Ohlin, at the national and micro-economic level, the competitiveness of actors will determine the direction and amount of trade flows. Trade will be dominated by exchanges that reflect the particular comparative advantages of given nation-states and also of given products. Destler confirms that "...in high-technology industries in which U.S. comparative advantage continued to increase, the U.S. trade surplus grew from $15 billion in 1973 to $52 billion in 1980."[3] In their final analysis, Kindleberger and Lindert affirm that "...most economists regard the Heckscher-Ohlin explanations of trade as broadly true."[4]

Clearly, interdependence theory emphasizes domestic economic causes of import penetration. The theory contends that if a NIC manufacturer can produce a particular commodity at a cheaper cost thus possessing a comparative advantage over a U.S. counterpart, we would expect the importation of that particular good to the U.S. market. Conversely, if a NIC's comparative advantage decreases, we would expect a decrease in import penetration in the U.S. Under the comparative advantage argument we would anticipate a positive relationship between a NIC's comparative advantage and the magnitude of U.S. import penetration. And furthermore, we would expect the relationship to be true at the commodity level of analysis. Delineated as such, the theory of interdependence suggests the following:

Hypothesis 1a: A change in comparative advantage will be associated with a change in the level of import penetration.

Hypothesis 1b: An increase in NIC's overall comparative advantage will be associated with an increase in the total U.S. import penetration, while a decrease in such advantage will be associated with a decrease in NIC's total penetration.

Hypothesis 1c: An increase in NIC's comparative advantage on a given level of processing will be associated with an increase in the magnitude of U.S. import penetrations for that export level, whereas, a decrease in such advantage will be associated with a decrease in import penetration.

The interdependence hypotheses are based on the assumption of harmonious economic interactions among different actors which will eventually produce the most efficient allocation of resources. Trade relations, to be mutually benefiting, are dictated by the economic principles of comparative advantages under a system of free trade. If a country possesses comparative advantage in a particular good, then that country will export that particular good to other countries which are less competitive. These flows of trade are (or ought to be) carried out in purely economic, market conditions--divorced from political regulations or interventions.

Dependency Hypotheses

Dependency theory begins with the premise that economic relations are essentially conflictual. There is no underlying harmony; one actor's gain is another's loss. In such a "zero-sum" international system which consists of a core, semi-periphery, and periphery, economic interactions are motivated by the logic of profitability. There is a tendency toward disequilibrium in the system since power and decisions are lodged in the financial and industrial core. Developing countries are conditioned by their relations to the international economy which is dominated by the developed countries.

More specifically, economic conditions and performances of core countries will determine the nature and amount of trade relations. Improved economic conditions in the developed countries will be directly related to the economic performance of these countries. If the core countries such as the United States experience expansion of their financial and industrial outputs, the NICs would experience expansion of their trade relations with the core countries. Conversely, if the core countries suffer economic decline, the NICs would simultaneously encounter diminished trade relations with those core countries.

Since dependent relationships exist within the broader, international capitalist system, general economic circumstances will have an undeniable effect on the NIC's trade relations with the core countries. Focusing on the international and intra-national economic factors, dependence perspective suggests these hypotheses:

Hypothesis 2a: A change in the United States' overall economic conditions will cause a change in NIC's overall import penetration into the United States.

Hypothesis 2b: An improvement in the overall economic condition of the United States will produce increased NIC's import penetration of U.S. markets, whereas a degenerating United States's economy will decrease the NIC's import penetration.

Hypothesis 2c: A change in international economic circumstances will determine the amount of the NIC's import penetration.

Hypothesis 2d: An improved international financial situation in a NIC will bring forth increased import penetration to the U.S. market, while a worsening situation will be associated with decreased import penetration of the NIC.

The dependency hypotheses of trade relations share common ground with the interdependence hypotheses. In explaining the causes of import penetrations, they are not directly competing hypotheses, rather they are complementary to one another. Both hold that trade relations are motivated by economic factors and are fueled by the notions of profitability. Nonetheless, the dependency hypotheses highlights international economic circumstance, whereas the interdependence hypotheses emphasize domestic economic causes. Specifically, since dependent economies are subjugated to the expansion or decline of dominant economies, NIC's import penetrations to the United States willbe determined by such conditions as the United States' employment rate, growth rate, etc. Further, since a dependent economy is a prisoner of the international capitalist system, international financial and monetary circumstances will guide the magnitude of trade relations.

Although dependency theory pays special attention to the structural and economic effects of dependent relationships, my main intention here is to investigate the reasons for import penetrations. Consequently, in this study, I am reluctant to make a further inquiry into the effects or purported distortions of dependent trade relations.

Mercantilist Hypotheses

Mercantilism claims that contrary to the attitude of liberalism and Marxism, international trade relations are in reality political relations. Huntington affirms that the prediction of the death of the nation-state by the interdependence theory is premature. He offers a contrary argument that, as the number and scope of trade activities increase, the value of one particular resource (i.e., power) almost exclusively under the control of a national government would also increase.[5]

What factors are important in determining trade relations between the U.S. and NICs from the mercantilist perspective? The foundation of the mercantilist description of trade relations is the state's thirst for power and wealth. Gilpin points out that the distributions of power and the nature of the political system are the major determinants of the system under which wealth is produced and distributed.[6] Since wealth can easily be converted to power, mercantilism attempts to manipulate economic arrangements and situations to maximize the state's own interest. Unmistakably, the primary actors are the nation-states and the fundamental factor is the nation-state's pursuit of national interests, especially those of national security interests.

Driven by its quest for power and national interest, the United States will, first of all, manipulate the trade relations with the NICs to maximize its own security interest. If the United States has a crucial security interest with a NIC, the United States may allow certain import penetrations from that NIC in order to maintain and maximize its national security interests. All things being equal, the saliency of the United States' security interests in a NIC will dictate the level of NIC's import penetration. Additionally, the United States and the NICs must contemplate their mercantilistic economic interests. The United States' economic interests as indicated by its import policies will have a significant input in regulating NIC's import penetration. A more restrictive U.S. import policy will curtail the NIC's import performances. A more liberal import policy, on the contrary, will boost their performances. Furthermore, the NIC's export policies will have a certain undeniable effect on their import penetration into the United States. If a particular NIC pursues a "strong" export policy, we would expect an increased import penetration, while a less robust export policy would produce a decreased penetration.

We would expect a positive relationship between the United States' security interest (i.e., "high" politics and the primary national goal) and the level of NIC's import penetration. Secondly, we would expect a significant relationship between the United States import policies (i.e., "low" politics, motivated by the mercantilistic notion of economic nationalism) and the NICs' import penetration. Thirdly, we would also anticipate a moderately strong relationship between the NICs' export policies and their import performances. The mercantilist hypotheses, for the trade relations between the United States and the Pacific Basin NICs, can be postulated as the following:

Hypothesis 3a: A shift in national interest considerations will bring forth a shift in NICs import penetration.

Hypothesis 3b: An increase in the U.S.'s security interest will be associated with an increase in NIC's import penetration whereas a decrease in such interest will be associated with a decrease in import penetration.

Hypothesis 3c: A more restrictive change in the United States' import policy, as indicated by increased trade disputes, will result in a decrease in NIC's import penetrations, whereas a more liberal change in such policy, as shown by decreased disputes, will produce an increase in import penetration.

Hypothesis 3d: A strengthening in NIC's export policies will produce a positive change in its magnitude of import penetrations to the United States, while a deterioration in the export policies will produce a reduction in import penetration.

The mercantilist hypotheses are based on the assumption that political factors are the primary determinants of international economic relations. The hypothesis 3b focuses on the national security interests and the hypotheses 3c and 3d concentrate on the mercantilistic economic interests of the states. It is assumed here that each nation state is motivated to maximize its national interests, whether or not this is at the expense of others. The mercantilist hypotheses that import penetration is caused by: (1) the convergence/divergence of national security interest between the United States and the NICs, (2) restrictive/liberal U.S. import policies, as indicated by an amount of trade disputes and (3) the strengthened or weakened NICs' export policies as approximated by a change in governmental role in export industries toward the NICs' penetration into the U.S. markets.

NOTES

1. Appendix A shows a complete listing of a number of commodities which have been categorized into six levels of processing. The list is derived from Firebaugh and Bullock's work. My categorization, however, is slightly different since I employed U.S. Commerce data, while Firebaugh and Bullock utilized the U.N. data. There were some tradeoffs in deciding which data set to use. The U.N. data is simpler but did not have all the NICs (e.g., Taiwan), whereas the U.S. Commerce data is more comprehensive, thus more cumbersome to work with.

2. Robert Gilpin, "The Nature of Political Economy," in *International Politics,* ed. Robert Art and Robert Jervis (Boston: Little Brown and Company, 1985), p. 279.

3. I.M. Destler, *American Trade Politics: System Under Stress.* (Washington, DC: Institute for International Economics, 1986), p. 41-42.

4. Charles P. Kindleberger and Peter H. Lindert, *International Economics.* 6th ed. (Homewood, IL: Richard Irwin, Inc, 1978), p. 30.

5. Samuel P. Huntington, "Transnational Organization in World Politics," *World Politics* 25 (1973), p. 363.

6. Gilpin, p. 286.

III
Methodology for Trade Research

This chapter presents the methodological issues regarding trade research. More specifically, the present chapter discusses the formulation of new trade variables and the methodological concerns of autocorrelations, diagnostic tests for autocorrelations, and correction of autocorrelation. After discussing the concept formation and the concerns of autocorrelations, the empirical methods for the present analysis will be presented and elaborated in order to provide a guideline in analyzing international trade relations.

FORMULATION OF TRADE DISPUTE VARIABLE

Over the years, political analyses of international trade have focused, either, on trade policies or the institutions of protectionism. The former analyses have dealt with tariff and non-tariff barriers of international trade, whereas the latter analyses have examined the institutions of trade policies.[1] In analyzing the trade relations between the Pacific Basin NICs and the United States, the present study offers a conceptualization of trade disputes, as a new indicator of U.S. import policy.

The formation of trade disputes is based on the assumption that trade disputes are filed as petitions with to the United States International Trade Commission (USITC). Created by Act of Congress as the United States Tariff Commission in 1916, the name was changed to the United States International Trade Commission by the Congress under the Trade Act of 1974. The Commission's major organizational mission is to "...[provide] technical assistance and advice to the President, the Congress, other Government agencies, and the public on international trade issues."[2] The

Commission is an independent, quasi-judicial, fact-finding agency that determines whether U.S. industries are materially injured by imports that benefit from various unfair and illegal activities from abroad.

Basically, there are four types of petitions filed against foreign competitors to the Commission: (1) adjustment assistance/escape clause, (2) unfair import practice, (3) anti-dumping, and (4) countervailing duties.

Petitions filed under adjustment assistance seek certain types of import relief, such as an increase in duties, establishment of quantitative restrictions, or specified types of adjustment assistance. For unfair trade petitions, the Commission may issue orders, excluding the articles which employ unfair methods of competition or unfair acts, from the entry into the United States, or issue cease and desist orders. Petitions for anti-dumping and countervailing duties are formal complaints by U.S. industries that imports are being sold at less than fair value or being subsidized by exporting governments. Upon investigation, the Commission may issue a special dumping or countervailing duty, if the Commission's determination is affirmative.

Procedures of Concept Formation

Petitions filed to the Commission from 1967 through 1985, aside from the four types mentioned above, are categorized in terms of: (1) date of filing, (2) date of settlement, (3) a final outcome, and (4) level of processing.

Each petition has been coded for its dates of filing and settlement. Since the present study deals with trade relations on an annual basis, both dates have certain meanings. The filing date of the petition signifies that a U.S. industry felt the need for certain adjustment, (i.e., import relief, desist order, or special duties), against foreign competition. A determination date, especially if the finding is affirmative, means that a specific corrective measure has been initiated against U.S. imports.

Upon investigation, the Commission determines an affirmative or negative finding for each petition. An affirmative finding denotes that there is a justifiable and reasonable indication of injury, while a negative finding means that the Commission finds no justifiable basis for its complaint. It is apparent that we need to distinguish those petitions which are reasonable, and the others which are not. As such, each petition is coded with respect to its final outcome--the Commission's affirmative or negative determination.[3]

Taken together, petitions filed with the U.S. International Trade Commission are categorized in terms of type of petition, dates filed and determined, a final determination, and a level of processing. This classification of petitions filed with the U.S. International Trade Commission constitutes the U.S. import policy, as expressed through trade disputes.

Table 3.1: Number of Petitions for Annual Totals and for Commodity Clusters by Filing Dates, 1967-1985

Year	TOT	L1	L2	L3	L4	L5	L6
1967	10	1	0	3	4	2	0
1968	8	1	0	1	5	1	0
1969	13	2	0	1	4	4	2
1970	58	3	0	5	30	5	15
1971	109	3	1	24	49	9	23
1972	87	4	4	13	30	8	28
1973	104	11	0	6	44	21	22
1974	65	2	3	6	29	7	18
1975	34	5	2	2	12	6	7
1976	30	2	2	6	5	7	8
1977	44	2	5	4	11	10	12
1978	69	5	3	9	22	19	11
1979	45	4	7	0	14	6	14
1980	143	39	4	5	52	13	29
1981	87	7	3	7	37	13	20
1982	263	7	5	4	212	15	20
1983	140	4	2	11	53	33	37
1984	168	10	4	4	94	30	26
1985	74	4	3	6	30	24	7
TOT	1551	116	48	117	737	233	299
(%)	100.0%	7.5%	3.1%	7.5%	47.5%	15.0%	19.3%

Table 3.1 presents the total numbers of petitions, from 1967 through 1985, categorized by their filing dates. For the time period between 1967

and 1985, a total of 1551 petitions was filed to the Commission as the formal complaints against foreign competitions. The largest number ofpetitions is filed during 1982, followed by 1984 and 1980. More specifically, from 1980 to 1985, the Commission received 875 petitions which is about 60 percent of all petitions. On the average, the highest percent of complaints were directed toward Level 4 commodities (47.5 percent), which consist of wearing apparel, footwear, and chemicals, followed by Level 6 commodities (19.3 percent), which include electrical, office, and telecommunication machines.

Table 3.2: Number of Affirmative Petitions for Annual Totals and for
Commodity Clusters by Filing Dates, 1967-1985.

Year	TOT	L1	L2	L3	L4	L5	L6
1967	3	0	0	1	1	1	0
1968	8	1	0	1	5	1	0
1969	9	0	0	0	4	3	2
1970	35	3	0	3	17	4	8
1971	34	3	0	14	8	3	6
1972	41	4	1	4	16	2	14
1973	41	7	0	2	15	11	6
1974	21	0	1	4	9	2	5
1975	15	3	1	1	6	2	2
1976	12	2	1	2	2	2	3
1977	20	0	5	2	2	4	7
1978	35	4	3	1	14	9	4
1979	22	1	7	0	6	3	5
1980	34	3	1	2	16	2	10
1981	42	3	3	1	23	5	7
1982	158	2	4	4	135	8	5
1983	83	1	2	4	46	15	15
1984	86	6	2	1	49	21	7
1985	50	4	0	1	26	15	4
TOT	749	47	31	48	400	113	110
(%)	100.0%	6.3%	4.1%	6.4%	53.4%	15.1%	14.7%

Table 3.2 shows the numbers of affirmative petitions in terms of their filing dates for the same time period. Between the years 1967 and 1985 there were a total of 749 affirmative petitions. This means that about half of all petitions (i.e., 48 percent) filed to the Commission for the time period have affirmative findings. The largest number of affirmative petitions is filed during 1982, followed by 1984 and 1983. Affirmative petitions during the time period from 1980 through 1985 account for more than 60 percent of all affirmative petitions. Once again, the bulk of affirmative petitions can be found for Level 4 (53.4 percent), Level 5 (15.1 percent), and Level 6 (14.7 percent) commodities.

Table 3.3: Percentage of Petitions for Six Commodity Clusters by Filing Dates, 1967-1985.

Year	L1	L2	L3	L4	L5	L6
1967	10.0%	0.0%	30.0%	40.0%	20.0%	0.0%
1968	12.5%	0.0%	12.5%	62.5%	12.5%	0.0%
1969	15.4%	0.0%	7.7%	30.8%	30.8%	15.4%
1970	5.2%	0.0%	8.6%	51.7%	8.6%	25.9%
1971	2.8%	0.9%	22.0%	45.0%	8.3%	21.1%
1972	4.6%	4.6%	14.9%	34.5%	9.2%	32.2%
1973	10.6%	0.0%	5.8%	42.3%	20.2%	21.2%
1974	3.1%	4.6%	9.2%	44.6%	10.8%	27.7%
1975	14.7%	5.9%	5.9%	35.3%	17.6%	20.6%
1976	6.7%	6.7%	20.0%	16.7%	23.3%	26.7%
1977	4.5%	11.4%	9.1%	25.0%	22.7%	27.3%
1978	7.2%	4.3%	13.0%	31.9%	27.5%	15.9%
1979	8.9%	15.6%	0.0%	31.1%	13.3%	31.1%
1980	27.3%	2.8%	3.5%	36.4%	9.1%	20.3%
1981	8.0%	3.4%	8.0%	42.5%	14.9%	23.0%
1982	2.7%	1.9%	1.5%	80.6%	5.7%	7.6%
1983	2.9%	1.4%	7.9%	37.9%	23.6%	26.4%
1984	6.0%	2.4%	2.4%	56.0%	17.9%	15.5%
1985	5.4%	4.1%	8.1%	40.5%	32.4%	9.4%

To examine the trend of petitions on an annual basis, Table 3.3 presents percentages of petitions broken down by the level of processing.

Over the years, as shown in Table 3.3, the highest percent of petitions are submitted for Level 4 commodities. For instance, more than 80 percent of all petitions filed during 1982 focused on Level 4 commodities. To a lesser extent, U.S. firms producing Levels 5 and 6 commodities have filed a considerable number of complaints against foreign competition. In fact, during 1976 and 1977, Level 6 commodities have the highest share of all petitions filed with the U.S. International Trade Commission. The trend of trade disputes suggests that U.S. industries that manufacture consume goods (e.g., wearing apparel and footwear) and semi-processed products (e.g., chemical products and semi-processed steel) have filed the highest number of complaints against foreign competition. They have filed the most complaints and made the most demands for specific governmental interventions to curtail the penetrations of U.S. markets by foreign competitors.

METHODOLOGICAL CONCERNS

The true behavioral relationship for the multivariate model is assumed to be

$$Y_i = \beta_1 X_{i1} + \beta_2 X_{i2} + \cdots + \beta_k X_{ik} + U_i \quad (3.1)$$

where Y_i is the dependent, or endogenous, variable for observation I; X_{ik} is the ith observation on the kth independent or exogenous variable; β_k is the coefficient for the kth variable or a constant slope for all I observation of the given variable X_k; and U_i is the stochastic element or random error for observation I.

The value of the dependent variable, Y_i is determined by adding a systematic component $(\beta_1 X_{i1} + \beta_2 X_{i2} + \cdots + \beta_k X_{ik})$ and a random component (U_i). The only observable quantities are the values of the explanatory variables and the final outcome for the dependent variable. It is not possible to observe the random component or the behavioral parameters. From our observations of Y_i and X_i's, we wish to estimate the parameters of β_1, β_2, and β_k.

For the multivariate model, it is necessary to make the following assumptions about the restrictions on the model and the U_i in order to produce the best linear unbiased estimator (BLUE).[4]

(1) $|r_{jk}| < 1.0$ for all $j \neq k$,
(2) Fixed X,
(3) $E(U_i) = 0$,
(4) $E(U_i^2) = U^2$ for all I, and
(5) $E(U_iU_j) = 0$ for all $I \neq j$.

Assumption (1) states that there are no exact linear combinations among the regressed exogenous variables (i.e., X_{i1}, X_{i2},...X_{ik}). Simply put, there is no perfect multicollinearity. Each of the exogenous variables has some considerable independent variation. Assumption (2) signifies that the values of X_{ik} are fixed and that only the random error terms, U_i's vary from one sample to another. Ideally, we could obtain many different samples for the values of X_{ik} and estimate the parameter estimates for each and every sample.

Assumption (3) indicates that since the error term is a random variable, its specific value for each observation is determined strictly by chance. For a large number of U_i's, the mean value or population mean would be zero. In other words, the error terms associated with each observation over all replication of the experiment have a zero mean.

Assumptions (4) and (5) pertain to the variances of error terms. The fourth assumption implies that all error terms have the same variance. This is the assumption of homoskedasticity that one does not expect the error term to be greater for higher values of the exogenous variables than for lower values.

The fifth assumption is that of no autocorrelation. All the error terms are assumed to be drawn independently of each other so that all the possible error terms associated with one observation are independent of, and thus uncorrelated with, the error terms of other observations.

For ordinary least square estimates (OLS) to be unbiased, Assumptions (1) to (3) must be true, and for OLS to be the BLUE (Best Linear Unbiased Estimator), Assumptions (4) and (5) must be satisfied. In addition, we need to make the assumption that the disturbance or stochastic error term is normally distributed around zero in order to allow statistical inference such as hypothesis testing on estimated coefficients for their significance.

Autocorrelation

Time-series analyses, e.g., international trade analyses, are commonly associated with a violation of Assumption (5), where error terms are correlated across different observations. This violation denotes that errors are not independently distributed. That is, when observations are made over time, the effect of the disturbance occurring at one period carries over into another period. Kmenta explains that

> Autocorrelation of the disturbances can be compared with the sound effect of tapping a musical string: while the sound is loudest at the time of impact, it does not stop immediately but lingers on for a time until it finally dies off. This may also be the characteristic of the disturbance, since its effect may linger for some time after its occurrence. But while the effect of one disturbance lingers on, other disturbances take place, as if the musical string were tapped over and over, sometimes harder than at other times.[5]

If the disturbances are autocorrelated, $E(U_t U_{t-s}) \neq 0$ (for some $t > s$.).[6] This means that the disturbance occurring at time t is related to the disturbance occurring at (t-s). A correction for autocorrelation requires more precise information about the nature and behavior of disturbances.

Most of the work on the correctional procedures of auto-correlation is based on the assumption that the regression disturbance follows a first-order autoregressive scheme, abbreviated as AR-1. If the disturbance of an observation (U_t) is correlated with the disturbance of the previous observation (U_{t-1}), we have

$$U_t = p\, U_{t-1} + E_t \quad \text{(for all } t) \quad (3.2)$$

where p is an autocorrelation coefficient, whose absolute value is less than one, and E_t is a normally distributed random error with zero mean and constant variance. It is assumed that E_t which is known as pure "white noise" is independent of U_{t-1}. That is, $E(E_t\, U_{t-1}) = 0$ for all t. This implies that each current disturbance (U_t) is equal to a portion of the preceding disturbance (U_{t-1}) plus a random effect represented by E_t.

Johnston notes that applying OLS to estimate a relationship with autocorrelated disturbances produces unbiased but inefficient estimation and yields invalid inference procedures.[7] It has been shown that the least squares estimators are unbiased even when the disturbances are autoregressive but the estimators are no longer BLUE.[8] Likewise, it has also been shown that the least square estimators are not asymptotically efficient, although consistent. The estimated variances of OLS estimators, i.e., *var(b)*, are biased and would cause a serious overestimation or underestimation of *t* statistics and significance levels in conventional inference procedures. To conclude, the consequences of autocorrelated disturbances are: (1) the least square estimators of the regression coefficients are unbiased and consistent but have no other desirable properties, and (2) the estimated variances of the least squares estimatorsare biased and conventionally calculated confidence intervals and tests of significance are not valid.[9]

Detection for Autocorrelation

It is a commonly accepted presumption that relationships estimated from observations over time often involve autocorrelated disturbances. Although there are several diagnostic procedures for detecting autocorrelation, the two most common types are: (1) the Durbin-Watson test and (2) visual diagnostics.[10]

The Durbin-Watson statistic is a straightforward diagnostic procedure for autocorrelation which makes use of the residuals from an OLS estimate of a model. It assumes that the residuals from the OLS estimation are consistent estimates of the underlying error terms and that they provide some indication of the structure of the error process in small samples. In the context of first order auto-correlation, we compute the value of the Durbin-Watson statistic (d) as

$$d = SUM(e_t - e_{t-1})^2 / SUM(e_t)^2, \quad (3.3)$$

where the e_t are residuals from OLS estimators.

As the sample size becomes large, the different ranges of summations in the numerator and the denominator have a diminishing effect and $d = 2(1 - p)$, where is the autocorrelation parameter. Johnston tells us that the range of d is from 0 to 4:

> $d < 2$ for positive autocorrelation of the e's;
> $d > 2$ for negative autocorrelation of the e's; and
> $d = 2$ for zero autocorrelation for the e's.[11]

Unfortunately, the distribution of the Durbin-Watson statistic depends not only on the sample size and number of coefficients being estimated, but also upon the sample values of the explanatory variables. Nevertheless, the distribution does have upper and lower bounds that are functions only of the sample size, the number of exogenous variables, and p.

There are two major drawbacks in using the Durbin-Watson statistic to test for the presence of autocorrelated disturbances. First, the test is valid strictly for nonstochastic explanatory variables. According to Johnston, it is not applicable if there is a lagged dependent variable, and it can be shown that the combination of a lagged Y variable and a positively autocorrelated disturbance term will bias the Durbin-Watson statistic upward and thus give misleading indications.[12] Second, there is some ambiguity if the test statistic falls between the upper and lowerbounds. The inconclusive range is an awkward problem and it becomes fairly large at low degrees of freedom, i.e., small sample sizes. One of the possible consequences is to accept the null hypothesis although it is false, which is a more serious problem than incorrectly assuming autocorrelation to be absent.

Another test for the presence of autocorrelated disturbances involves visual diagnostics. Chatfield states that "anyone who tries to analyze a time series, without plotting it first, is asking for trouble."[13] A typical visual diagnostic is to plot OLS residuals against time. If the residuals tend to run in certain streaks, it is necessary to analyze it further in more a sophisticated manner by plotting the autocorrelation function which is known as the correlogram.

The autocorrelation function (ACF) is a set of correlation coefficients between U_t and U_{t-1}, U_t and U_{t-2}, and so on, as a function of the lag involved. As mentioned earlier, the AR-1 autocorrelated disturbance is written as $U_t = pU_{t-1} + E_t$, for all t, and this gives the autocorrelation function as

$$p_k = r_k/r_0, \quad k = 1, 2,... \quad (3.4)$$

Since $|p| < 1$ and $p > p^2 > p^3$, the autocorrelation function will decay exponentially. Furthermore, the correlogram will geometrically decline when p_k is positive and it will oscillate in sign if p_k is negative.

In addition to the ACF, the partial autocorrelation function (PACF) is an important tool to describe the stochastic properties of autocorrelated disturbances. It is noted that the kth partial autocorrelation coefficient measures the correlation between a stochastic process y_t and y_{t-k}, given $y_{t-1},...,y_{t-k+1}$. In other words, the partial autocorrelation coefficient $\{r_{pk}\}$ measures the excess correlation at lag k which is not accounted by an AR (*t-k*) models and when plotted against the autocorrelation coefficient (p_k) gives the partial autocorrelation function.[14]

Customarily, it is assumed that the regression disturbance follows a first-order autoregressive process (AR-1). However, if we assume an AR-1 when in fact the disturbances have a more complicated structure, i.e., AR-2, AR-3, then we may have estimates that are even less efficient than the OLS.[15] Thus to determine the correct autoregressive process, it is necessary to examine and visually inspect the correlograms of the partial autocorrelation functions. Chatfield affirms that values of partial autocorrelation coefficients r_p which are outside the two standard error limits are significantly different from zero.[16] It can be shown that the PACF of an AR (p) process 'cuts off' at lag *p* so that the 'correct' order is assessed as that value of p beyond which the sample values of $\{r_{pj}\}$ are not significantly different from zero. This means that the partial autocorrelations have a cutoff point at lag *p*. Visually, the PACF correlogram will be truncated beyond the confidence intervals for the particular autoregressive process. For instance, if it truncates only at the first lag, then AR-1 model may be appropriate. If it truncates at both the first and second lags, then the true model may be a combination of the first and second autoregressive processes.

As the general guidelines for interpreting the correlograms, Chatfield describes the following tendencies of autocorrelation coefficients:

(1) A random series--If a time series is completely random, then for the large N, *rk*=0 for all non-zero values of *k*. This means that 19 out of 20 of the values of *rk* can be expected to lie between two standard error limits.

(2) short-term correlation--This is characterized by a fairly large value of r_1 followed by 2 or 3 more coefficients which, while significantly greater than zero, tend to get successively smaller. Values of r_k for longer lags tend to be approximately zero.

(3) Alternating series--If a time series has a tendency to alternate, with successive observations on different sides of the overall mean, then the correlogram also tends to alternate. The value of r_1 will be negative, whereas the value of r_2 will be positive as observations at lag 2 will tend to be on the same side of the mean.

(4) Non-stationary series--If a time series contains a trend, then the values of r_k will not come down to zero except for very large values of the lag.[17]

(5) Seasonal fluctuations--If a time series contains a seasonal fluctuation, then the correlogram will also exhibit an oscillation at the same frequency.[18]

Chatfield cautions that a visual inspection of the correlogram is not an easy task--it takes some training and experience to detect the presence of autocorrelation and determine the correct order of autoregressive process.[19]

Correction for Autocorrelation

To apply an appropriate estimation procedure for models with autocorrelated disturbance, we must (1) determine the order of autoregressive process, and (2) transform or adjust the data, if necessary. As we have discussed in the previous section, the correct specification of disturbances is an essential requirement for an efficient autoregressive estimator. Furthermore, it may be necessary to transform or adjust the data to remove any trend or seasonal fluctuations. If the evidence from the correlogram suggests that the data contain a seasonal trend, it is necessary to modify the series through a transformation or an adjustment.

The common types of data transformations include logarithmic and square root transformation. As pointed out by Chatfield, there are three main reasons for making a transformation. The first is to stabilize the variance. If there is a trend in the series and the variance appears to increase with the mean then it may be necessary to transform the data. The second type is to make the seasonal effect additive. If there is a trend in the series and the size of the seasonal effect appears to increase with the mean then it may be advisable to transform the data so as to make the seasonal effect constant. And finally, it may be required to transform to make the data normally distributed.[20]

Adjustment procedures are usually performed on the data with long-term trends. If the data contain a long term trend, the values of autocorrelation coefficients will not come down to zero except for very large values of the lag. The data contain non-stationary series and one must remove this trend prior to running any analysis. One of the most common adjustment techniques for non-stationary series is to transform the data through "differencing." Differencing is a special type of filtering, which is particularly useful for removing a seasonal or annual trend. This procedure simply differences a given time series until it becomes stationary. As noted by Kmenta, taking the first difference is sufficient to remove any trend.[21] One rarely needs to take second or higher differences. After taking the first difference, the adjusted data should be checked again by plotting the ACF and PACF to detect the presence and determine the order of autoregressive process, if any.

Once the correct diagnostics are made concerning the autoregressive process, we can apply a number of estimation procedures. The most widely accepted procedure is known as the generalized least squares (GLS) estimation, pioneered by Cochrane-Orcutt. For the first autoregressive process, suppose that the equation to be estimated is

$$Y_t = \beta_0 + \beta_1 X_t + U_t, \quad (3.5)$$

where $U_t = pU_{t-1} + E_t$. By multiplying this equation with the known value of p, we get

$$p\,Y_{t-1} = p\beta_0 + p\beta_1 X_{t-1} + p\,U_{t-1}. \quad (3.6)$$

Subtracting the second equation from the first yields

$$Y_t - pY_{t-1} = \beta_0(1-p) + \beta_1(X_t - pX_{t-1}) + (U_t - pU_{t-1}), \quad (3.7)$$

and this can be rewritten as

$$Y_t^* = \beta_0^* + \beta_1 X_t^* + V_t. \quad (3.8)$$

Now V_t will no longer be autocorrelated and the least squares estimators are best linear unbiased estimators.

When p is unknown, we need to estimate the value of p with the least squares residuals. The least squares estimator of p is given as

$$\hat{p} = SUM(e_t e_{t-1})/ SUM(e_{t-1})^2, \quad (3.9)$$

where e_t and e_{t-1} denote OLS residuals. Applying OLS to equation (3.8) after replacing p with $\hat{p}$ is known as the Cochrane-Orcutt two-step method. Kmenta asserts that this procedure requires two successive applications of OLS: the first to obtain $\hat{p}$ and the second to obtain estimates of β_0 and β_1 and their estimated standard error. If the two-step procedure is repeated until convergence, the resulting estimators of β_0 and β_1 are known as the Prais-Winsten iterative estimators.[22] These estimated general least squares (EGLS) can be shown to be best linear unbiased estimators and asymptotically consistent and efficient.

To conclude about the EGLS estimation, Kmenta affirms that (1) unless the value of p is quite small (say, less than 0.3), the Prais-Winsten estimators perform better than the OLS estimators, (2) generally, the iteration procedure helps in improving the performance of the estimators, and (3) the tests of significance, even when performed with transformed data, may be unreliable.[23]

The discussion of the various methodological concerns has disclosed that there are several prerequisites for analyzing international trade relations. In order to avoid methodological traps and since the analysis will be based on annual data, we need to determine if the data contain any annual trends. If so, the data must be adjusted by implementing the appropriate procedures, such as differencing. In addition, we need to determine whether or not the data contain autoregressive disturbances. If the diagnostic procedures of the Durbin-Watson statistics and the autocorrelation function confirm the presence of autocorrelations, we would need to specify the correct autoregressive process (AR-1, AR-2), by examining the partial autocorrelation function. With the correct diagnosis of disturbances, we would then apply the appropriate estimation procedures, such as the Prais-Winsten iterative procedures.

More specifically, there are four possible types of analyses based on the stationary of series and on the presence/absence of autocorrelation: (1) stationary series with no autocorrelation, (2) non-stationary series with no autocorrelation, (3) stationary series with autocorrelation, and (4) non-stationary series with autocorrelation. For detection of non-stationary series and autoregressive disturbances, the correlograms of autocorrelation functions and the Durbin-Watson statistics will be used as the essential diagnostic tools. Similarly, the specification of the autoregressive process will be determined by the correlograms of the partial autocorrelation functions.

NOTES

1. See William R. Cline, *The Future of World Trade in Textiles and Apparel* (Washington, D.C.: Institute for International Economics, 1987); William R. Cline, *Exports of manufactured From Developing Countries* (Washington, D.C.: Brookings Institution, 1984); Robert E. Baldwin, *The Political Economy of U.S. Import Policy* (Cambridge, MA: MIT Press, 1985); Judith Goldstein, "The Political Economy of Trade," *American Political Science Review* 80 (1986): 161-184; Pietro S. Nivola, "The New Protectionism: U.S. Trade Policy in Historical Perspective," *Political Science Quarterly* 101 (1986): 577-600; and John S. Odell,"The Outcomes of International Trade Conflicts: The US and South Korea, 1960-1981," *International Studies Quarterly* 29 (1985) : 263-286.

2. United States International Trade Commission, *Annual Report* (Washington, D.C.: International Trade Commission, 1967-1988), p. 1.

3. This is not, always, an easy task. The Commission's investigation process may take as little as 60 days or as long as 3 to 4 years. Often times, length of investigation is affected by court litigation for licence agreement and trademark and changes in Commissioners.

4. Eric A. Hanushek and John E. Jackson, *Statistical Methods for Social Sciences* (New York: Academic Press, 1977), p. 46-54.

5. Jan Kmenta, *Elements of Econometrics* (New York: Macmillan Publishing, 1986), p. 299.

6. For relationships estimated from observations over time, the variables are given a subscript t (for time) rather than the subscript I that is used in the general case.

7. J. Johnston, *Econometric Methods* (New York: McGraw-Hill, 1984), p. 310.

8. Johnston, p. 311.

9. Kmenta, p. 311.

10. For example, there are King's locally optimal bounds test, the Berenblut-Webb test, Geary's sign change test, the Breusch-Godfrey test, and the Wallis test for fourth-order autocorrelation.

11. Johnston, p. 315.

12. Ibid., p. 316.

13. C. Chatfield, *The Analysis of Time Series: An Introduction* (London: Chapman and Hall, 1985), p. 7.

14. George Judge, et al *The Theory and Practice of Econometrics* (New York: John Wiley and Sons, 1985), p. 7.

15. Robert F. Engle, "Specification of the Disturbances for Efficient Estimation." *Econometrica* 41 (1974): 225-38, in examining the specification of the disturbances for efficient estimation, compared theestimates derived from autoregressive least squares (ALS) and OLS. He found that only when ALS represents a minor misspecification of the true disturbance process is it necessarily better than OLS. Otherwise, OLS is superior and vastly more efficient.

16. Chatfield, p. 69.

17. Broadly speaking, a time series is said to be stationary if there is no systematic change in mean, if there is no systematic change in variance, and if strictly periodic variation has been removed.

18. Chatfield, p. 25-30.

19. Ibid.

20. Ibid., p. 14-16.

21. Kmenta, p. 321-322.

22. Ibid., p. 315-319.

23. Ibid., p. 323.

IV
Operationalization and Models of Analysis

Chapter II presented the causes of and hypotheses about import penetration suggested by three competing theoretical perspectives. To test these causal factors, this chapter will provide the operationalizations of the variables and the functional forms of the models under investigation. The variables to be defined and to be studied in the functional forms include: (1) import penetration, (2) comparative advantage, (3) macroeconomic condition, (4) United States' import policy, (5) NICs' export policy, and (6) United States' national security interest. After defining these variables, I will present the functional forms of the individual and integrative models of import penetration, that is, interdependence, dependence, mercantilist, and composite models. Subsequently, I will discuss the expected results of these models in accordance which the suggestions of the respective theoretical perspectives.

OPERATIONALIZATION OF THE VARIABLES

Import Penetration
Import penetration denotes the amount of imports from country A to country B. Generally, it means the actual value of commodities transferred across national boundaries. The amount or the value of imports from the NICs into the U.S. can be measured as a national total for a NIC and also as a total for each of six levels of processing, classified in terms of the amount of labor skills and capital necessary to produce the commodities. For the time period of the study, import penetration will be estimated as follows: (a) the total amount of commodities imported from an individual

NIC, measured as a percent share of imports, into the United States, and (b) the amount of imports from an individual NIC, measured as a percent share of imports, for a particular "level of processing" of commodities. Furthermore, the Pacific Basin regional totals will be computed as the aggregate of NICs' national totals, and their totals for six commodity clusters.

The official U.S. import statistics are compiled initially by the Bureau of the Census in terms of the commodity classifications in "Tariff Schedules of the United States Annotated" (TSUSA). These classifications are rearranged as the codes of Schedule A, which is based on the Standard International Trade Classification (SITC) of commodities imported into the United States.[1] Customarily, every item that is imported into the United States is assigned a 7-digit identification code. The 7-digit codes, which account for more than 10,000 items, are part of a series of six progressively broader product categories up to the 1-digit level which separates U.S. imports into 10 general categories.

For this study, I have decided to use a 2-digit SITC code which classifies imported commodities into 64 categories. This particular code allows sufficient variations of commodities to be meaningful while maintaining a data set of manageable size.[2]

Each of the 64 two-digit categories is assigned a particular processing code, following the Firebaugh and Bullock method of classifying commodities which distinguishes three levels of primary products and three levels of manufactured goods. For example, live animals were assigned to the first level of processing, organic chemicals to the fourth level, and office machines to the sixth level. This categorization presupposes that there is a qualitative difference between different types of imports. Since each commodity serves diversified consumers and since each faces different U.S. manufacturers, it seems reasonable to assume that each cluster of imported commodities from NICs will produce a distinct impact and penetration pattern.

Subsequently, the import penetration variables are constructed as follows:

NICPUS--NICs' total imports as a percent of total U.S. imports.
NICPUSL1-L6--NICs' total imports for each level of processing.
SIGPUS--Singapore's total imports as a percent of total U.S. imports.
SIGPUSL1-L6--Singapore's total for each level of processing.
KORPUS--Korea's total imports as a percent of total U.S. imports.
KORPUSL1-L6--Korea's total for each level of processing.

HKPUS--Hong Kong's total imports as a percent of total U.S.imports.
HKPUSL1-L6--Hong Kong's total for each level of processing.
TAWPUS--Taiwan's total imports as a percent of total U.S. Imports.
TAWPUSL1-L6--Taiwan's total for the level of processing.

Comparative Advantage

As a concept, comparative advantage offers a micro-economic rationale for import penetration. Essentially, it is based on a particular actor's endowment with productive factors. Generally, comparative advantage is determined by the amounts of human and capital resources required to produce certain commodities.

Previous analyses have shown that comparative advantage can be measured in a number of ways.[3] For example, "value added per worker" as a proxy measure, indicates labor intensity of production. High values added indicate low labor intensity, and vice versa. The other measures include "physical capital per worker" which is the ratio of physical capital such as plant and equipment to employment in the industry, and "human capital per worker" which is the value of education and skills, or human capital, in the work force, measured by using the difference between the average wage and the wage of unskilled labor.[4]

For the Pacific Basin NICs, the lower labor costs of production offer a commonly accepted rationale for their comparative advantages over the United States. If a NIC manufacturer can produce a particular commodity with cheaper labor costs than a U.S. counterpart, then that NIC manufacturer has a comparative advantage for that commodity.

Labor costs are computed from the wage and output data available from national statistics and also from United Nations' publications. The United Nations' *Industrial Statistics Yearbooks* from 1967 through 1985 provide a consistent basis for computing comparative advantage measures for Singapore, Korea and Hong Kong, while the measure for Taiwan is computed based on its national statistics. This *Industrial Statistics* contains estimates of wages and salaries including all payments in cash or in kind made to employees and operatives during the reference year.[5]

From these data, comparative advantages are computed as the total of labor costs divided by the total value of industrial outputs for particular commodities. The following commodities represent the corresponding levels of processing:

Level 1--Food, Food product, and Tobacco.
Level 2--Textile and Leather.
Level 3--Glass and Nonferrous metals
Level 4--Wearing apparel, Footwear, and Steel.
Level 5--Chemical, Plastic, and Metal products.
Level 6--Machinery and Electrical Machinery.

Based on this commodity classification, the labor cost for each level is computed by taking the average of the selected commodities. This cost for each NIC is then divided by the cost in the United States for the same commodities. Computed as such, comparative advantage is a relative measure indicating the differences between the costs to produce those commodities for the NICs and the United States. A smaller value in comparative advantage represents an advantage for a NIC over the United States, while a larger value indicates a comparative disadvantage. The variables for comparative advantages are coded as follows:

NICCA--NICs' average comparative advantage.
NICCAL1-L6--NICs' average comparative advantage for each level of processing.
SIGCA--Singapore's average comparative advantage.
SIGCAL1-L6--Singapore's average comparative advantage for each level of processing.
KORCA--Korea's average comparative advantage.
KORCAL1-L6--Korea's average comparative advantage for each level.
HKCA--Hong Kong's average comparative advantage
HKCAL1-L6--Hong Kong's average comparative advantage for each level.
TAWCA--Taiwan's average comparative advantage.
TAWCAL1-L6--Taiwan's average comparative advantage for each level.

Macroeconomic Conditions

Macroeconomic conditions are relatively easy concepts to define. Major economic indicators, which illuminate international and domestic economic conditions are readily available and extensively quantified. However, the problem for the present study is deciding which macroeconomic indicators to use. Dornbusch and Frankel note that the most important (as a potential macroeconomic determinant) is probably the exchange rate: an overvalued currency induces a rise in import competition.[6] In addition to the exchange rate, macroeconomic conditions are reflected by the real production (GNP) growth rate. Simply put, an improved core economy at the macro level will produce a higher consumption rate, holding the other factors constant.

Another possible indicator of macroeconomic conditions of the core country is the rate of unemployment. Unemployment rates represent the domestic reactions to import penetrations. A high unemployment rate indicates that the domestic labor forces are being overwhelmed by the foreign competition. A lower unemployment rate signifies that the core economy is maximizing its available labor force for overall expansion.

The analysis will use the dollar exchange rate, the United States' GNP growth rate, and the rate of unemployment to evaluate the import penetrations from the NICs. The variables for macroeconomic conditions are coded as follows:

NICER--NICs' average exchange rates over the U.S. dollar.
SIGER--Singapore's avg. exchange rates over the U.S. dollar.
KORER--Korea's avg. exchange rates over the U.S. dollar.
HKER--Hong Kong's avg. exchange rates over the U.S. dollar.
TAWER--Taiwan's avg. exchange rates over the U.S. dollar.
USGNP--U.S. Gross National Product growth rate.
USUEP--U.S. unemployment rate.

U.S. Import Policy

As an indicator of U.S. import policies, trade disputes would have a certain impact on NICs' import penetrations. If a NIC is charged with dumping a particular good, the penetration of the disputed good may be substantially curtailed. Conversely, the absence of trade disputes will be associated with unrestricted import penetrations. A restrictive import policy, as indicated by an increase in trade disputes, is more likely to produce a decreased penetration, whereas a liberal import policy, as shown through a decrease in trade disputes, will lead to an increased import penetration.

Data on trade disputes is available from the United States International Trade Commission (USITC) which publishes an annual report of petitions filed against foreign competitors. The petitions are filed and categorized in terms of (1) adjustment assistance/escape clause, (2)

unfair import practice, (3) anti-dumping, and (4) countervailing duties.
Domestic U.S. manufacturers may request import relief assistance
under the adjustment assistance and escape clause petitions. The Trade
Expansion Act of 1962 provides means whereby industries or firms that
are seriously injured or threatened with serious injury because of
increased imports may seek relief. According to the *Annual Report*,
following an investigation and affirmative finding by the Commission, the
President may,

> ...under specified circumstances, increase rates of
> duty or impose other restrictions on imports which are
> causing or threatening to cause serious injury to a
> domestic industry, negotiate orderly marketing
> agreements with foreign countries, or certify adversely
> affected firms or groups of workers as eligible to apply
> for adjustment assistance.[7]

The adjustment assistance may take several forms. Actual adjustment
assistance may be provided in terms of loans, technical assistance, and tax
benefits to firms for unemployment compensation and retraining.
Beginning in 1976, Section 201 of the Trade Act of 1974 provides
the means whereby relief can be sought by domestic manufactures under
the escape clause. Relief may be sought by a trade association, a firm, a
certified or recognized union, or a group of workers. When petitioned, the
Commission determines whether an article is being imported into the
United States in such increased quantities as to be a substantial cause of
serious injury or threat to the domestic industry. The *Annual Report*
affirms that

> If the Commission determines in the affirmative, it
> must find the amount of the increase in, or imposition of,
> any duty or restriction on such article which is necessary
> to prevent or remedy such injury, or recommend the
> provision of adjustment assistance to firms, workers, or
> communities.[8]

The Commission conducts investigation under section 337 of the
Tariff Act of 1930 to determine whether unfair methods of competition
and unfair acts exist in the importation of articles into the United Sates.
The Commission determines whether there is a tendency to substantially

injure a domestic industry, efficiently and economically operated, in the United States. The *Annual Report* states that if the Commission finds a violation, it can issue orders excluding the violating goods from entry into the United States, unless it determines that such orders should not be issued in view of a public-interest consideration. Commission orders go into effect 60 days after issuance unless disapproved by the President.[9]

Section 201 (a) of the Antidumping Act, 1921, makes provision to deal with imported articles sold at less than their fair values. The *Annual Report* asserts that

> ...whenever the Secretary of Treasury advises the Commission that a class or kind of foreign merchandise is being, or is likely to be, sold in the United States or elsewhere at less than its fair value, the Commission shall determine within 3 months whether an industry in the United States is being or is likely to be injured, or is prevented from being established, by reason of the importation of such merchandise. At the conclusion of its investigation, the Commission notifies the Secretary of the Treasury of its determination.[10]

If the Commission determines in the affirmative, the Secretary of Treasury issues a finding that dumping has occurred, and the described imports become subject to special dumping duties.

In addition, the U.S. antidumping law, which is set forth in sections 731-740 of the Tariff Act of 1930, provides for the levying of special duties to offset sales at less than fair value (LTFV) by foreign producers. According to the *Annual Report*,

> The Department of Commerce must determine whether an imported article is being sold at less than fair value, and the Commission must determine whether an industry in the United States is materially injured or threatened with material injury, or whether the establishment of an industry in the United States is materially retarded, by reason of alleged sales at less than fair value. In these investigations, the Commission is obliged to examine a domestic industry in order to assess the impact of imports on the industry's economic health.[11]

Section 303 of the Tariff Act of 1930 provides the provision dealing with countervailing duties directed toward U.S. imports. The *Annual Report* states that:

> ...whenever any country, dependency, colony, province, or other political subdivision of government, person, partnership, association, cartel, or corporation shall pay or bestow, directly or indirectly, any bounty or grant upon the manufacture or production or export of any article or merchandise manufactured or produced in such country, dependency, colony, province, or other political subdivision of government, then upon the importation of such article or merchandise into the United States, whether it is imported directly from the country of production or otherwise and whether it is imported in the same condition as when exported from the country of production or has been changed in condition by remanufacture or otherwise, there shall be levied and paid, in all such cases, in addition to any duties otherwise imposed, a duty equal to the net amount of such bounty or grant, however the same be paid or bestowed.[12]

Effective January 1, 1980, the Trade Agreements Act of 1979 became the law governing responses to countervailing duties. The *Annual Report* states that the new statute added a requirement. The Commission must determine that an injury to a domestic industry has occurred before imposition of countervailing duties.[13] In addition, the benefit of a Commission's injury determination is extended to subsidy cases involving merchandise subject to duty provided that the merchandise originates in a signatory to the Subsidies Code of the General Agreement of Tariffs and Trade (GATT).

The *Annual Report* states that under title VII of the Tariff Act of 1930, as added by the Trade Agreements Act of 1979, the Commission

> ...conducts preliminary and final investigations to determine whether there is a reasonable indication that (in preliminary investigations) or whether (in final investigations) a U.S. industry is materially injured or threatened with material injury, or the establishment of such an industry is materially retarded, by reason of imports of

merchandise which is being sold at less than fair value or is benefiting from foreign subsidies. The Department of Commerce determines whether dumping or subsidies exist and, if so, the margin of dumping or amount of the subsidy.[14]

The Commission finding concerns only whether there is injury by reason of that dumping or subsidy. If the Commission finds that such dumping or subsidies are causing damage to a U.S. industry, the Commission recommends an amount of dumping or countervailing duties equal to the amount of the foreign subsidy.

The above categories of petitions, compiled by the Commission, are aggregated annually for the overall total and the totals for six processing clusters of commodities. Although a petition indicates a domestic demand for protectionism and an alleged or an actual unfairness from the foreign manufactures, petitions have varying degrees of success and importance. As such, each petition is coded with respect to its date of filing, date of settlement, and final outcomes (an affirmative or negative finding). Trade disputes, as an approximation of the U.S. import policy, are coded as follows:

TD1TOT--The total number of petitions coded by the date filed.

TD1L1-L6--The total number for each level.

TD1YTOT--The total number of petitions filed coded by the date filed and with affirmative findings.

TD1YL1-L6--The total for each level.

TD2TOT & TD2L1-L6--The total number of petitions coded by the date decided & the total for each level.

TD2YTOT & TD2YL1-L6--The total number of petitions coded by the date decided with affirmative findings & the total for each level.

NICs' Export Policy

Export policies are those policies actively promoted by the NICs' governments in pursuit of market access in the United States. Theoretically, since trade relations are bilateral, an inclusion of NIC export policies is essential in providing a complete explanation of U.S./NICs trade relations. Okita maintains that "effective government policies in NICs buttressed by close cooperative efforts by government, industry, and academia are the most important reason for the recent NICs' development."[15] The World Bank Study affirms that Korean industrial policy is notable for the prominent role of government in the economy, the boldness of policy changes, and extraordinary results. The study adds that Korea's export takeoff would not have been possible without decisive and innovative government policies.[16]

It appears that effective government policies are consolidated around financial issues. Generally, an effective export policy denotes strong governmental assistance in exporting production. Governmental assistance may be in the form of direct government subsidies, low interest rate loans to export manufactures, and lower taxes for the manufacturers. Effective government policies can be viewed as a function of the resources and intentions of government to finance, and thus to facilitate, exports and export industries.

Governmental assistance data are usually confidential and apparently very difficult to obtain. Due to the unavailability of this data, export policies of NICs will be approximated from the rates of domestic capital formation and domestic governmental expenditure. Okita claims that the NICs recent development is accountable to "...a high rate of investment, specifically investment backed by dramatically higher domestic saving rates (or domestic capital formation)."[17] Given this, rates of capital formation are adopted as the proxy measure of export policies, since they are relatively reasonable indicator of the amount of investment capital available to the NICs (and thus the NICs' governments) for investment or export purposes.

The rates of government expenditure are also used to measure export policies of the NICs. These rates of expenditure reflect the financial resources a NIC government's disposal. Before a NIC's government can assist export productions, it must have financial resources to support its intentions. A higher rate of government expenditure implies a higher financial capacity to assist, while a lower rate denotes a decreased capacity to promote export production. The data for each NIC's domestic capital formation and government expenditure are adopted from the United Nations' *National Accounts Statistics* for the time period of the study. The NICs' export policies are coded as follows:

NICCF--NICs' average domestic capital formation as the percent of gross domestic products.
SIGCF--Singapore's capital formation.
KORCF--Korea's capital formation.
HKCF--Hong Kong's capital formation.

TAWCF--Taiwan's capital formation.
NICGE--NICs' average government expenditure as the percent of gross domestic products.
SIGGE--Singapore's government expenditure.
KORGE--Korea's government expenditure.
HKGE--Hong Kong's government expenditure.
TAWGE--Taiwan' government expenditure.

National Security Interest

According to the realist vision, national security interest is the most important political determinant of economic relations. A high politics of national security is the primary source of concern about NICs' import penetration. Conventional realism stipulates that a state will manipulate its economic arrangements to promote its security interests. From this posture, Sneider asserts that "American security interests are [as] deeply engaged in Asia as they are in Europe...American interests remain constant--to prevent hostile powers from expanding their control over the region and to maintain sufficient power to thwart any direct or indirectthreat to the United States."[18]

National security interest is a complex phenomenon and it has acquired many meanings over the years. Keohane and Nye affirm that "national interests will be defined differently on different issues, at different times, and by different governmental units."[19] For the present study, the U.S. security interest in a particular NIC will be approximated by measuring the amount of U.S. aid given to that NIC. In other words, we can define the American security interest as the amount of U.S. foreign aid given to a NIC on an annual basis. The amount of U.S. economic and military aid is thus a direct indication of the degree and magnitude of American security interests bestowed on a particular NIC. In this way, the American security interest is coded as follows:

NICUSTA--The average of the total U.S. aid given to the NICs.
SIGUSTA--Singapore's total aid from the United States
KORUSTA--Korea's total aid from the United States
HKUSTA--Hong Kong's total aid from the United States
TAWUSTA--Taiwan's total aid from the United States

MODELS OF IMPORT PENETRATION

Models of import penetration present functional forms for analysis based on the causal factors suggested by the dominant theoretical perspectives. The interdependence model emphasizes a microeconomic cause of import penetration. Following the classical theory of international trade, the functional form of the interdependence model consists of the "labor" comparative advantage of NICs. Comparative advantage is measured as an absolute difference in labor costs between a NIC and the United States in producing a particular commodity. The interdependence model will be tested on three levels of analysis: (1) a regional level, an aggregate sum for the all NICs, (2) a national level, a national total for each NIC, and (3) a commodity level, a total for each of six clusters of commodities.

The dependency model focuses on the macroeconomic determinants of import penetration. The model will be comprised of the exchange rate, GNP growth rate and unemployment rate of the United States. Exchange rates between the NIC's currency and the U.S. dollar reflect the overall financial condition of the international capitalist system. The United States' GNP growth and unemployment rates indicate a change in the core nation's overall economic conditions and the rate of expansion to which the peripheries (the NICs economies) are subjected.

The mercantilist model is concerned with the self-centered policies of trading nations. This model stems from the notion that a nation-state seeks to manipulate trade relations to maximize its own interests. Each nation-state pursues a distinct set of objectives under the rubric of national interest. The functional form of the mercantilist model will simultaneously consider the national interests of the United States and those of the NICs. It will include, (1) trade disputes which approximate U.S. import policy toward the NIC, (2) NIC's domestic capital formation and government expenditure to indicate NICs' export policy toward the United States, and (3) U.S. total aid to the NIC as an indicator of U.S. security interest in that NIC.

Contrary to the interdependence hypothesis, the dependency and mercantilist hypotheses are not explicitly concerned with the micro or commodity level of analysis. Their emphasis is on the aggregate or macro level of analysis. These hypotheses do not preclude, however, the possibility that might exist at the commodity level of analysis. Whether this focus on macro relationship is caused by the nature of their theoretical frameworks or simply by a lack of attention to the micro level is unclear. Testing the dependency and mercantilist hypothesis at the commodity level of analysis may provide some information regarding their lack of precision. The results of the tests may demonstrate the inherent limitations of dependency and mercantilist hypotheses in dealing with the micro level of analysis. On the other hand, the tests may lead to some tangible suggestions as to how to change or modify their assumptions and arguments to perhaps better address the present circumstances. In sum, these tests may lead to a synthesis of theories or suggestion for a new theory of international political economy.

Interdependence Model

The interdependence perspective is based on the fact that different commodities require different factors for production, and different countries have different quantities of factors of production. A country will possess a comparative advantage in good *X* if the country is relatively well endowed with factors that are used intensively in the production of *X*. A country will export the commodity that uses intensively its relatively abundant resources.

If a NIC manufacturer can produce a particular commodity at a lower cost, thus possessing a comparative advantage over a United States counterpart, we would expect the importation of that particular commodity into the U.S. market. A change in comparative advantage will be associated with a change in the level of import penetration. Particularly, an increase in a NIC's overall comparative advantage will be associated with an increase in its overall import penetration, whereas adecrease in such an advantage will be linked to a decrease in U.S. import penetration. Moreover, an increase in a NIC's comparative advantage on a given level of processing will causes an increase in U.S. import penetration for that level of processing. The functional form of the interdependence model can be stated as

$$Y_i = \beta_0 + \beta_1 X_{i1} + U_i \qquad (4.1)$$

where Y_i = Import Penetration, and
X_{i1} = "Labor" Comparative Advantage.

Because "labor" comparative advantage is measured as an absolute difference between the labor costs in producing a commodity, we would expect a negative relationship between a NIC's labor cost and its import penetration. We would anticipate that a lower labor cost will covary with a higher propensity to achieve import penetration of that commodity. Conversely, a higher labor cost for a particular commodity will be associated with less likelihood of that commodity being imported into the U.S. market.

Dependency Model

The dependency perspective is based on the idea that trade relations are conditioned by the developed economies in particular, and by the international system in general. For a NIC, the types and amounts of import penetration will be conditioned and defined by United States economic situations. If the U.S. economy experiences an expansion in financial and industrial output, a NIC would also experience an expansion in its exports to the United States.

In addition, since the dependent relationships between the NICs and the United States exist within the broader international capitalist system, international economic indicators such as the dollar exchange rates will have an undeniable impact on the NIC's imports into the U.S. market. The importations of commodities from the NICs into the United States will be determined by the U.S. macroeconomic conditions and by circumstances surrounding the international capitalist system. Thus, this perspective maintains that

$$Y_i = \beta_0 + \beta_2 X_{i2} + \beta_3 X_{i3} + \beta_4 X_{i4} + U_i \qquad (4.2)$$

where Y_i = Import Penetration,
X_{i2} = Dollar Exchange Rate,
X_{i3} = U.S. GNP Growth Rate, and
X_{i4} = U.S. Unemployment Rate.

Accordingly, we would expect a positive relationship between the NICs' exports to the United States and their dollar exchange rate. A higher dollar exchange rate means that a NIC's own currency (i.e., Korea's won, Taiwan's dollar, etc.) is under-valued relative to the U.S. dollar, thus it is cheaper to import commodities into the U.S. market. A lower exchange rate denotes that a NIC's currency is over-valued relative to the U.S. dollar, making its commodities more expensive in the U.S. market.

We would also expect a positive relationship for the GNP growth rate. A positive growth rate, an expansion in the United States economy, will be associated with increased import penetration, while a negative growth rate will coincide with a lower, more sluggish rates of penetration. The U.S. unemployment rate would be negatively related to the NIC's import penetration. If the United States domestic labor market is damaged by the NIC's imports, we would expect a reduced demand for those imports. And if the United States experiences full employment, we would expect an increased demand for commodities from the NICs.

Mercantilist Model

The mercantilist perspective is based on the idea that domestic political interests under the rubric of national interests will shape the trade relations between nations. The trade policies and political concerns of participating states will determine the exchanges of commodities across national boundaries. In particular, self-interested United States import and NIC export policies, coupled with overriding security interests, will overshadow the NICs' import penetrations.

Driven by its quest for wealth and power, the United States will manipulate trade relations with the NICs to maximize its own economic and political interests. First, the United States' mercantilistic economic interests, as indicated by its import policies, will have a significant impact on the NIC's import penetration. A restrictive U.S. import policy, defined as an increase in trade disputes between the United States and a NIC, would curtail the level of import penetration, while a liberal policy, demonstrated as a decrease in trade disputes, would assist in promoting a higher rate of NIC's import penetrations.

Second, the United State's security interest in a particular NIC would determine that NIC's propensity to penetrate the U.S. market. The amount of economic and military assistance denotes the U.S. security interest and commitment to that NIC which, in turn, allows a higher rate of import penetration. A lower or decreasing amount of United States assistance to a NIC signifies that the U.S. security interests and commitments are dissipating with respect to that particular NIC, curtailing its rate of penetration.

Third, the mercantilist economic interests of the NICs, as shown by their export policies, will be causally related to their propensities toward import penetrations in the U.S. market. A NIC's export policy, defined as domestic capital formation and government expenditure will be positively related to import penetration. An increase in a NIC's domestic capital formation and government expenditure will be a necessary condition for an increase in import penetration. A decreased capital formation and expenditure will cause a reduction in the NIC's import penetration.

The functional form of the mercantilist model can be written as follows:

$$Y_i = ß_0 + ß_5X_{i5} + ß_6X_{i6} + ß_7X_{i7} + ß_8X_{i8} + U_i \qquad (4.3)$$

$$\text{where} \quad \begin{aligned} Y_i &= \text{Import Penetration,} \\ X_{i5} &= \text{Trade Dispute,} \\ X_{i6} &= \text{Domestic Capital Formation,} \\ X_{i7} &= \text{Government Expenditure, and} \\ X_{i8} &= \text{United States Total Aid.} \end{aligned}$$

For this model, negative relationship is expected between NIC's import penetration and trade dispute. Simply put, more trade dispute (i.e., friction) mean fewer import penetration. From increased domestic capital formation, government expenditure, and total U.S. aid, we would expect a positive relationship with a NIC's import penetration. In other words, increased domestic capital, government expenditure and U.S. assistance will have a positive impact on a NIC's propensity to successfully export to the United States. Holding other factors constant, export stimulating policies by a NIC, coupled with a convergence of security interests, will allow increased commodity penetration into the U.S. market.

Composite Model

The composite model of import penetration pools the determinants of the three individual models of international trade into a single equation. Alike the individual models, the composite model will be analyzed from the regional, national, and commodity level of analysis. The functional form of the composite model can be written as:

$$\begin{aligned} Y_i = &\, ß_0 + ß_1X_{i1} + ß_2X_{i2} + ß_3X_{i3} + ß_4X_{i4}\ ß_5X_{i5} + ß_6X_{i6} \\ &+ ß_7X_{i7} + ß_8X_{i8} + U_i \end{aligned} \qquad (4.4)$$

$$\text{where} \quad \begin{aligned} Y_i &= \text{Import Penetration,} \\ X_{i1} &= \text{"Labor" Comparative Advantage,} \\ X_{i2} &= \text{Dollar Exchange Rate,} \end{aligned}$$

X_{i3} = U.S. GNP Growth Rate,
X_{i4} = U.S. Unemployment Rate,
X_{i5} = Trade Dispute,
X_{i6} = Domestic Capital Formation,
X_{i7} = Government Expenditure, and
X_{i8} = United States Total Aid.

The rationale for running the composite model analysis is to perform an additional, critical test on the individual models and their determinants of the NICs' import penetration into the U.S. market. The composite analysis will focus on the consistency of the individual models--the interdependence, dependency, and mercantilist--as an adequate explanation of NICs' import penetration. That is, if an individual model analysis yields a strong and significant result, we would expect to find a similar result for the composite model. On the other hand, if two results are inconsistent, we would seriously question the model's theoretical and empirical adequacy.

Moreover, the composite model analysis may offer some concrete suggestions as to "how to" conceptualize international trade relations, probing the possibility of a new theory building and/or a theoretical synthesis of international trade.

For the composite model, we would expect the same directions of the relationships between the determinants of the individual models and the NICs' import penetration into the United States, as previously discussed. In short, the comparative analysis of the individual and the composite models has an important implication for the evaluation of the causes of the Pacific Basin NICs' import penetration into the U.S. market. It will serve as the secondary evaluation of the individual models and their determinants of import penetration.

NOTES

1. For more detailed description of commodity classifications, see the "explanation of statistics" in *U.S. General Import (FT 155)* published by the U.S. Department of Commerce.

2. This seems to be a conventional procedure. For example, Edward E.Leamer, *Sources of International Comparative Advantage: Theory and Evidence* (Cambridge, MA: MIT Press, 1984), has based his analysis on the data set consisting of 10 aggregations from 61 two-digit SITC codes.

3. See especially William R. Cline, *Exports of Manufactured From Developing Countries* (Washington, DC: Brookings Institution, 1984).

4. Ibid., p. 46-47.

5. The payments include the following items: (a) direct wages and salaries, (b) remuneration for time not worked, © bonuses and gratuities, (d) housing allowances paid directly by the employer, and (e) payments in kind.

6. Rudiger Dornbusch and Jefferey A. Frankel, "Macroeconomics and Protection," in *U.S. Trade Policies in a Changing World Economy*, ed. Robert H. Stern (Cambridge, MA: MIT Press, 1987).

7. U.S. International Trade Commission,*Annual Report* (Washington, D.C.: International Trade Commission, 1973), p. 5.

8. U.S. International Trade Commission,*Annual Report* (Washington, D.C.: International Trade Commission, 1976), p. 4.

9. U.S. International Trade Commission,*Annual Report* (Washington, D.C.: International Trade Commission, 1982), p. 11.

10. U.S. International Trade Commission, *Annual Report* (Washington, D.C.: International Trade Commission, 1979), p. 14.

11. U.S. International Trade Commission, *Annual Report* (Washington, D.C.: International Trade Commission, 1981), p. 4.

12. U.S. International Trade Commission, *Annual Report* (Washington, D.C.: International Trade Commission, 1980), p. 20.

13. Ibid., p. 3.

14. U.S. International Trade Commission, *Annual Report* (Washington, D.C.: International Trade Commission, 1983), p. 3.

15. Saburo Okita,"Pacific Development and Its Implications for the World Economy," in *The Pacific Basin: New Challenges for the United States*, ed. James Morley (New York: Academy of Political Science, 1986), p. 24.

16. World Bank, *Korea: Managing the Industrial Transition* (Washington, DC: The World Bank, 1988), p. 29.

17. Okita (fn. 12), p. 24.

18. Richard Sneider, "United States Security Interest," in *The Pacific Basin: New Challenges for the United States*, ed. James Morley (New York: Academy of Political Science, 1986), p. 77

19. Robert O. Keohane and Joseph S. Nye, *Power and Interdependence: World Politics in Transition*, 2nd edition, (Boston: Little, Brown and Company, 1989), p. 35.

V

Results of the Analyses

Based on the functional forms and the methodological concerns discussed earlier, this chapter presents and interprets the results of the analyses. First, I will discuss the results of the descriptive statistics, emphasizing the essential variables' central tendencies and dispersions. Second, the results of the unadjusted OLS estimation will be reported, appraising the predictive powers of the individual models. Third, the results of the visual diagnostics will be presented to identify the correct functional forms for the analysis. Fourth, the results of the estimations on the adjusted data will be presented and elaborated to evaluate the explanatory and predictive powers of the individual models for the regional, national and commodity levels of analysis. Finally, a comparative analysis of the individual and the composite models will be provided to determine the individual models' overall performance and their "goodness of fit" in explaining the NICs' import penetration into the United States. The presentation and discussion of the results will focus on the explanatory powers of the individual models and their determinants at the various stages of estimations--yielding some new insights into how to think about international trade relations.

INTERPRETATION OF RESULTS

Descriptive Analysis Result

The present study tests the models of import penetration based on the data from the Pacific Basin NICs for the period between 1967 to 1985. The data set consists of 99 variables, including: 35 import penetration variables, 35 comparative advantage variables, 5 exchange rate variables,

Table 5.1 : Descriptive Analysis Results for Select Variables

Variable	Mean	Std. Dev.	Minimum	Maximum	n
NICPUS	6.95	2.42	2.793	11.31	19
SIGPUS	0.61	.36	.052	1.233	19
KORPUS	1.69	.74	.396	2.900	19
HKPUS	2.09	.27	1.621	2.538	19
TAWPUS	2.56	1.19	.569	4.748	19
NICCA	60.53	7.13	50.8	72.8	18
SIGCA	64.78	9.15	49.4	84.2	19
KORCA	53.55	4.58	46.8	63.8	19
HKCA	65.90	4.34	58.5	73.7	18
TAWCA	59.75	14.61	41.1	78.2	19
NICER	108.51	11.24	98.0	135.4	19
SIGER	104.67	16.12	88.2	128.7	19
KORER	105.12	38.69	56.0	179.8	19
HKER	121.62	20.47	98.1	164.6	19
TAWER	102.61	3.80	95.5	106.3	19
USGNP	2.76	2.41	-2.5	6.4	19
USUEP	6.40	1.84	3.5	9.7	19
TD1TOT	81.63	63.61	8.0	263.0	19
NICGE	54.79	1.57	51.9	57.2	18
SIGGE	58.08	4.27	52.2	67.4	18
KORGE	36.98	2.81	32.1	42.0	18
HKGE	36.98	2.81	32.1	42.0	18
TAWGE	87.08	5.55	75.3	97.9	18
NICCF	158.28	24.68	112.1	197.3	18
SIGCF	208.96	47.90	111.3	282.4	18
KORCF	149.12	17.41	109.2	180.3	18
HKCF	132.48	30.98	82.8	188.2	18
TAWCF	142.51	20.30	116.9	192.0	18
NICUSTA	69.83	60.49	-66.0	197.0	19
SIGUSTA	5.79	31.57	-53.0	93.0	19
KORUSTA	248.05	144.27	58.0	698.0	19
HKUSTA	2.53	11.12	-14.0	32.0	19
TAWUSTA	57.68	135.27	-255.0	392.0	19

2 variables for United States GNP growth and unemployment rates, 7 trade disputes variables, and 5 each for government expenditure, capital formation, and U.S. total aid.

Table 5.1 presents the descriptive statistics (e.g., mean, standard deviation, minimum value, and maximum value) for the select variables. On the average, the Pacific Basin NICs account for about 7 percent of the total U.S. imports. Taiwan has the highest share with 2.56 percent, followed by Hong Kong (2.09 percent), Korea (1.69 percent), and Singapore (.61 percent). For comparative advantage, the NICs' average labor cost is about 61 percent of the United States' labor cost. Korea has the highest advantage over the United States with 53.33 percent, Taiwan is the second with 59.75 percent, followed by Singapore (64.78 percent) and Hong Kong (65.90 percent).

The dollar exchanges rates show that Hong Kong has the weakest currency relative to the U.S. dollar with the average index of 121.6, Korea is the second with 105.1, Singapore is the third with 104.7, and Taiwan has the strongest dollar exchange rate with the index value of 102.6. For the period between 1967 and 1985, the U.S. gross national products have grown at 2.76 percent annually and unemployment rates have averaged to 6.4 percent.

American domestic industries, interest groups, and trade unions--among others--have filed about 82 petitions per year to United States International Trade Commission. The actual numbers of petitions range from the minimum of 8 petitions and the maximum of 263 petitions. On the average, the NIC's government expenditure is approximately 55 percent of that of the United States. The Taiwanese government has the highest spending tendency with 87.1 percent, surpassing Singapore (58.1 percent), Korean and Hong Kong (each with 37.0 percent). For domestic capital formations, the NICs, on the average, account for about 158 percent of the U.S. capital formations. Individually, Singapore has the highest capital formation rate with 209 percent, Korea is the second with 149 percent, Taiwan and Hong Kong averaged 143 percent and 132 percent, respectively. For U.S. military and economic assistance, Korea is the largest recipient with the annual average of $248 millions, Taiwan is the next largest with $58 millions, while Singapore and Hong Kong have received about $6 and $3 millions each.

Unadjusted Ordinary Least Squares Estimation

For the individual models of import penetration, I ran ordinary least squares (OLS) to estimate their suggested effects. In this section, the results of unadjusted OLS estimations will be presented in terms of the percent of estimates with the correct signs to provide a general comparison of each model.[1] The actual coefficient estimates will be presented and discussed in details in the later sections after the visual diagnostics and subsequent data adjustment.

The results in Table 5.2 show that comparative advantage, U.S. unemployment rate, and trade dispute are expected to have negative relationships with NICs' import penetration, whereas dollar exchange rate, U.S. GNP growth rate, NIC's government expenditure and capital formation, and U.S. total assistance are expected to be positively related with the import penetration.

Table 5.2: Expected Results and Percentage of Unadjusted
OLS Estimates with Correct Signs for All Equations*

Model	Variable	Expected Result	OLS Result	(%)
INT	CA	$\beta < 0$	28.6	28.6
DEP	ER	$\beta > 0$	62.9	
	USGNP	$\beta > 0$	45.7	
	USUEP	$\beta < 0$	37.1	48.6
MER	TD1	$\beta < 0$	37.1	
	GE	$\beta > 0$	60.0	
	CF	$\beta > 0$	60.0	
	USTA	$\beta > 0$	57.1	53.6

*Note that INT=Interdependence, DEP=Dependency, and MER= Mercantilist Model.

The unadjusted OLS estimates for the individual models show that the mercantilist model has the highest overall prediction with 53.4 percent of estimates with the expected signs.[2] The second highest is the dependency model with 48.6 percent and the last is the interdependence model with 28.6 percent of estimates predicted correctly. Among the individual determinants, the U.S. dollar exchange rate has the highest percent of estimates with the expected sign with 62.9 percent, followed by the NIC's government expenditure and capital formation with 60.0 percent each.

Table 5.3 present the OLS estimates for the regional and the national level of analysis. Table 5.3 shows that none of the NICs' comparative advantage has the correct sign. It appears that the interdependence model does not explain the variations of the NICs import penetration when aggregated into a summary figure.

Table 5.3: Percentage of Unadjusted OLS Estimates with Correct
Signs for Each NIC (%)

Model	SIG	KOR	HK	TAW
INT	0.0	0.0	0.0	0.0
DEP	33.3	66.6	66.6	33.3
MER	50.0	75.0	0.0	0.0

For the dependency model, the dollar exchange rate and the U.S. GNP growth rate are positively related with NICs' import penetration as expected. In fact, 100 percent of exchange rates and 86 percent of U.S. growth rate have correct OLS estimates. At the national level, dollar exchange rate is predicted correctly for Korea and Hong Kong, and U.S. growth rate is correct for all NICs. In other words, at the national level, the dollar exchange rate explains Korea and Hong Kong situations better than Singapore and Taiwan, confirming the speculation that Korea and Hong Kong have pursued the exchange rate policies to keep the values of their currencies down (i.e., devalue) relative to the U.S. dollar to maintain their products' competitiveness in the U.S. market, while Taiwan and Singapore did not. For the U.S. GNP growth rate, it seems that all the NICs are affected by the changes in the U.S. economy conditions. An improving U.S. economy, as indicated by a higher GNP growth rate, has a positive impact on NICs' import penetration, whereas, a worsening U.S. economy curtails NICs' import penetration. This is especially true for Taiwan, Singapore, and Korea, but not for Hong Kong.

At the regional level, the mercantilist model predicted 71 percent of all coefficient estimates. Specifically, the NICs' government expenditure and capital formation display 86 percent of estimates predicted correctly. This supports the stipulation that much of NICs' import penetrations are internally generated by the NICs themselves. As expected, a higher government expenditure and capital formation is directly related to an increase in the NICs export into the United States. At the national level, the model shows 31 percent of correct coefficient estimates. The model has the highest prediction rate for Korea (75 percent), followed by Singapore (50 percent), while generating the worst fits for Hong Kong and Taiwan (0 percent).

Table 5.4 presents the percentage of the unadjusted OLS estimates with the correct sign for the commodity level of analysis. For the commodity level of analysis, the comparative advantage shows some predictability with 33.3 percent of estimates showing the expected signs. The dependency model, as a whole, has correctly predicted 47.8 percent of the unadjusted OLS coefficient estimates. The mercantilist model has the highest overall prediction with 55.8 percent. For Levels 1, 2 and 5 commodities, the mercantilist model has the highest predictive ratio among the individual models. For Levels 3 and 6 commodities, the dependency model registered the highest percentages with 60 percent and 53 percent of the expected signs. The interdependence and mercantilist model have the highest percent for Level 4 commodities with 60 percent of estimates with correct signs.

Table 5.4: Unadjusted OLS Estimates with Correct Signs for Commodity Level

Model	Levels of Processing (%)						Overall (%)
	L1	L2	L3	L4	L5	L6	
INT	20.0	40.0	40.0	40.0	60.0	40.0	33.3
DEP	33.3	40.0	60.0	53.3	40.0	46.7	47.8
MER	60.0	55.0	55.0	60.0	60.0	45.0	55.8

The OLS estimation on the unadjusted data has shown that for the regional and the commodity level of analysis the mercantilist model has the best predictive power among the individual models. Concurrently, the dependency model has the superior predictive power at the national level of analysis. Somewhat surprisingly, the interdependence model is the worst individual model, predicting none of the estimates correctly at the regional and the national level, while explaining only a small variation (i.e., 33.3 percent) at the commodity level of analysis. According to the unadjusted OLS estimations, import penetrations from the NICs can be attributed to the determinants of the dollar exchange rate, the U.S. GNP growth rate, the trade disputes, the NIC's government expenditure and capital formation, and the United States total assistance.

Visual Diagnostic Result

Upon examining the Durbin-Watson statistics and the scatter plots of residuals from the unadjusted OLS estimations, there appears to be some annual trends and/or autocorrelations. To determine whether the data contain any non-stationary series and/or autoregressive disturbances, the correlograms of the autocorrelation functions of all 99 variables are examined as suggested by Chatfield.

The correlograms of the autocorrelation functions have confirmed the suspicion from the Durbin Watson statistics and the residual plots that the data contains certain annual trends and autoregressive disturbances. To determine the annual trends, the correlograms were checked to see if the values of autocorrelation coefficients move toward zero at the small or at the large value of the lag. The series which move toward zero at relatively large lags (e.g., non-stationary series) have been adjusted by taking the first differences. After taking the first differences, the correlograms are plotted on the adjusted series to see if these adjustments have successfully removed the annual trends.

The visual diagnostic of the correlograms and the adjustment procedures disclosed that 22.2 percent of the data had stationary series with no autocorrelation, while 72.7 percent had non-stationary series caused by the annual trends. None of the variables had just autocorrelation, but 5 variables have both non-stationary series and autocorrelations.[3]

In addition, to determine the correct autoregressive process for those five variables with autocorrelations, the correlograms of the partial autocorrelation functions are constructed and interpreted. These correlograms have disclosed that the partial autocorrelation coefficients are "cut off" at the first lag, telling us that correct error specification is the first order auto-regressive process.

Based on the visual diagnostics, the appropriate functional forms (equations) for the present analyses are summarized in Table 5.5.

Table 5.5 shows that only 1 equation out of 105 total equations belongs to unadjusted OLS estimation. 85 equations (81 percent of all equations) require adjusted OLS estimation and 19 equations (18 percent)

Table 5.5: Correct Equations for the Analysis Based on the
            Visual Diagnostics

Model	OLS(D=0)	OLS(D=1)	EGLS*
INT			
NIC	0	7	0
SIG	1	6	0
KOR	0	5	2
HK	0	7	0
TAW	0	7	0
DEP			
NIC	0	0	7
SIG	0	7	0
KOR	0	6	1
HK	0	0	7
TAW	0	6	1
MER			
NIC	0	7	0
SIG	0	7	0
KOR	0	6	1
HK	0	7	0
TAW	0	7	0
TOTAL	1	85	19

*Note that EGLS is Estimated Generalized Least Squares.

necessitate EGLS estimation. The individual models have varying numbers of the appropriate functional forms. The interdependence model requires 32 adjusted OLS, 2 EGLS and 1 unadjusted OLS estimation. The dependency model necessitates 19 adjusted OLS, 16 EGLS, and zero unadjusted OLS estimation. The mercantilist model requires 34 adjusted OLS and 1 EGLS estimation.

Estimation on the Adjusted Data

After the data adjustment based on the diagnostic tests, the second OLS estimation and also the EGLS estimation were run. The results from these estimations are quite different from the previous, unadjusted OLS estimation.[4] Table 5.6 displays the results of the adjusted estimations in terms of the percentages of estimates with the expected signs for the overall, the aggregated regional, and the national levels of analysis.

Table 5.6: Estimates from the Adjusted Data with Correct Signs for All Equations, Regional and National Level (%)

Mod	Var	Overall Result		Regional Level		National Level	
INT	CA	62.9	62.9	85.7	85.7	50.0	50.0
DEP	ER	45.7		71.4		50.0	
	USGNP	65.7		85.7		100.0	
	USUEP	31.4	47.6	14.3	57.1	0.0	50.0
MER	TD1	31.4		14.3		25.0	
	GE	54.3		57.1		50.0	
	CF	37.1		28.6		0.0	
	USTA	51.4	43.6	71.4	34.2	50.0	31.3

According to Table 5.6, the interdependence model has the highest overall percentage (62.9 percent) of estimates with the expected signs for the adjusted estimations. This is a direct opposite of the unadjusted OLS estimation, where the interdependence model had the lowest predictive rate with 28.6 percent of estimates with the correct signs. The second highest is the dependency model with 47.6 percent and the lowest overall is the mercantilist model with 43.6 percent of estimates with the expected signs.

At the regional level, the interdependence model has the highest percentage of estimates with the correct signs with 85.7 percent. Once again, this is a drastic change since none of the unadjusted OLS estimates had the correct sign. The dependency model has the second highest prediction rate with 57.1 percent of estimates predicted correctly. However, without including the U.S. unemployment rate, the dependency model would have tied with the interdependence model for the highest predictive percentage. The mercantilist model has the lowest percentage of estimates with the correct sign with 34.2 percent, dropping from the 71.4percent of the unadjusted OLS estimation.

At the national level, the interdependence and dependency model correctly estimated 50 percent of their estimates, while the mercantilist model only predicted 21.3 percent correctly. Among the individual variables, U.S. GNP growth rate registered the highest rate with 100 percent of estimates with the expected signs.

Table 5.7 summarizes the percentages of the adjusted estimates with the expected signs for the commodity level of analysis. For the commodity level of analysis, once again, the interdependence model has the highest predictive rate with 63.3 percent of estimates with the expected signs. The dependency model has the second highest rate with 42.2 percent, and the mercantilist model has the lowest predictive rate with 45 percent of estimates with expected signs. For the individual levels of commodities, the interdependence model has the highest percentage of estimates with the correct sign for Levels 2, 4, 5 and 6 commodities. The mercantilist model has the highest predictive ratio for Level 1 commodities. The dependency model has the highest percentage for Level 3 commodities. Throughout the six clusters of commodities, the interdependence model has yielded the highest predictive rate followed by the dependency model and then by the mercantilist model.

Table 5.7: Estimates of the Adjusted Data with Correct Signs for Commodity Level

Model	Levels of Processing (%)						Overall (%)
	L1	L2	L3	L4	L5	L6	
INT	0.0	100.0	40.0	80.0	80.0	80.0	63.3
DEP	33.3	40.0	53.3	40.0	46.7	66.7	46.7
MER	50.0	50.0	50.0	40.0	40.0	40.0	45.0

The results of the estimations on the adjusted data are radically different from those of the unadjusted OLS estimation. Although the results of the dependency and mercantilist model are not drastically different, the results of the interdependence model are significantly different from the unadjusted results. In fact, the interdependence model has consistently transcribed the highest percentages of estimates with the correct sign. For the overall, regional, national and commodity level of analysis, the interdependence model has the highest predictive rates. In light of the results from the unadjusted OLS estimation, this is indeed an alteration of the results (in terms of the coefficient estimates with the expected signs) that requires a closer inspection.

Aside from the percentages of estimates with the expected signs that I have discussed thus far, the succeeding set of tables presents the actual coefficient estimates in order to delineate the exact nature and strength of relationships between the NICs' import penetration and the theoretical determinants of the individual models. The coefficient estimates for the interdependence model are presented in Tables 5.8 and 5.9.

Table 5.8: Coefficient Estimates for the Interdependence Equations at Regional and National Level.

Variable	bi_1	Standard Error	t-ratio
NICCA	-.110	.097	-1.143
SIGCA	.002	.004	.328
KORCA	.002	.016	.134
HKCA	-.013	.021	-.595
TAWCA	-.049**	.021	-2.327

Table 5.9: Coefficient Estimates for the Interdependence Equations for the Regional Aggregate Level.*

Level	bi_1	Standard Error	t-ratio
NICCA L1	.001	.004	.031
NICCA L2	-.001	.011	-.089
NICCA L3	-.023	.027	-.861
NICCA L4	-.025	.087	-.285
NICCA L5	-.035	.063	-.558
NICCA L6	-.039	.080	-.492

*All coefficients not significantly different from 0.00 at .05 level.

Table 5.8 shows that--at the aggregated regional and national level-- NICs, Hong Kong and Taiwan display negative relationships between their comparative advantages and import penetrations, as expected, while the results for Singapore and Korea are inconsistent indicating the positive (rather than negative) coefficient estimates. In addition, only one estimate (TAWCA) is significantly different from zero at .05 significance level.

Table 5.9 shows that with the exception of Level 1 commodities, all of the coefficients have the expected signs. The results confirm the interdependence hypothesis that comparative advantage is negatively related to the commodity penetrations from the NIC's. However, this finding is in conclusive. None of the coefficient estimates are statistically significant. The estimated coefficients are not significantly different from zero at .05 significant level.

Tables 5.10 and 5.11 present the estimated coefficients of the dependency determinants of import penetration.

Table 5.10: Coefficient Estimates for Dependency Equations at Regional and National Level

	ER	GNP	UEP
	b_{i2}	b_{i3}	b_{i4}
	Stand. Error	Stand. Error	Stand. Error
	T-Ratio	T-Ratio	T-Ratio
NICs	.086**	.334**	.447
	.040	.135	.259
	2.133	2.471	1.730
SIG	-.006	.019	.022
	.004	.015	.030
	-1.554	1.239	.732
KOR	-.004	.024	.027
	.008	.047	.090
	-.461	.501	.300
HK	.009	.052	.079
	.006	.041	.084
	1.473	1.267	.937
TAW	.100***	.152**	.144
	.024	.040	.079
	4.126	3.788	1.820

**Significantly different from 0.00 at .05 level.
***Significantly different from 0.00 at .01 level.

Table 5.10 displays the coefficient estimates for the aggregated regional and national, and the commodity clusters. It shows that the U.S. dollar exchange rates are positively related to import penetration for the NICs, Hong Kong, and Taiwan. More precisely, overvaluation of the U.S. dollar has a significant impact on import penetrations for the NICs, Hong Kong, and Taiwan, while Singapore and Korea show inconsistent results, suggesting that their import penetrations continue to increase in spite of the dollar devaluations. As expected, the U.S. GNP growth rate is positively related to import penetration for the NICs and all four individual NICs. Once again, the coefficients are significant only for the NICs and Taiwan. Additionally, for all four NICs, the U.S. unemployment rate yields the inconsistent result, showing that the rate is positively related to the NICs' import penetration into the United States.

For the commodity level of analysis, as shown in Table 5.11, the results are similar to those from the regional and national estimates. The dollar exchange rate has the expected direction of relationship for the Level 1, 3, 4, and 6 commodities. The GNP growth rate has the most consistent results for all levels of commodities except for the second level. The unemployment rate shows the consistent estimate only for the second level of commodities. The remaining levels have inconsistent results. These results, however, are not conclusive, since all coefficients are not significantly different from zero at .05 α level.

Table 5.11: Coefficient Estimates of the Dependency Equations
for Regional Aggregates at Commodity Level

NIC	ER	GNP	UEP
	b_{i2}	b_{i3}	b_{i4}
	Stand. Error	Stand. Error	Stand. Error
	T-Ratio	T-Ratio	T-Ratio
L1	.020	.064	.068
	.012	.042	.081
	1.648	1.519	.842
L2	-.018	-.135	-.080
	.024	.086	.164
	-.756	-1.570	.338
L3	.045*	.044	.058
	.027	.089	.171
	1.68	.488	.338
L4	.049	.295	1.455
	.111	.413	.795
	.442	.715	1.832
L5	-.044	.286	.782
	.073	.274	.527
	-.595	1.044	1.483
L6	.007	.142	.139
	.075	.252	.483
	.094	.565	.289

*Significantly different from 0.00 at .10 level.

Tables 5.12 and 5.13 present the estimated coefficients of the mercantilist determinants of import penetration, (i.e., trade dispute, NIC's domestic capital formation, NIC's government expenditure, and United States total assistance) for the regional, national and commodity clusters. Table 5.12 discloses that at the aggregated regional and national levels, trade dispute is negatively related as expected only for Hong Kong. The other NICs have positive coefficient estimates telling us that a restrictive U.S. import policy, as indicated by an increase in trade disputes fails to curtail the import penetration. The NICs' penetrations increased even during the times of growing trade disputes. The NIC's domestic capital formations, contrary to the hypothesized direction, display a uniform negative relationship with their import penetrations. In other words, the pattern of the NIC's import penetration has little to do with its domestic savings rate, at least for the aggregated national totals.

Table 5.12 also shows that the NIC's government expenditure is positively related--as expected--for the aggregated NICs, Singapore and Korea, but not so for Hong Kong and Taiwan. Increased imports into the United States from Singapore and Korea are at least partially determined by the expansions in their government expenditures, while for Hong Kong and Taiwan the government expenditures are irrelevant in explaining their import penetrations. The U.S. security interest as approximated through the U.S. total assistance has positive impacts for the aggregated NICs, Korea and Hong Kong. However, the results in Table 5.12 indicate that the relationship is negative for Singapore and Taiwan, which means that their exports into the United States have not been affected by the U.S. total assistance.

As displayed in Table 5.13, for the commodity level of analysis, the trade dispute variable, at only one level of commodity (Level 1), has the hypothesized direction of relationship and the remaining levels have inconsistent (positive) relationships. For NIC's domestic capital formation, only two levels (Levels 2 and 3) show the expected direction of relationship. NIC's government expenditure has a positive impact on the NIC's import penetration for Levels 1, 2 and 3 commodities, while the U.S. total military and economic aid has the correct coefficients for Levels 1, 2, 4 and 5 commodities. Among those coefficients with the correct direction of relationship, only one coefficient (U.S. total aid for Level 4) is significantly different from the null hypothesis of ß=0. Overall, the mercantilist determinants of import penetration have a higher predictive power for the lower level (Levels 1 to 3) commodities than the higher level (Levels 4 to Level 6) commodities. The mercantilist determinants

have 66.7 percent of coefficients with the consistent results for the lower
level commodities, while only 16.7 percent of coefficients are consistent
for the higher level commodities.

Table 5.12: Coefficient Estimates for the Mercantilist Equations at
Regional and National Level

NIC	TD1	CF	GE	USTA
	b_{i5}	b_{i6}	b_{i7}	b_{i8}
	S.E.	S.E.	S.E.	S.E.
	t-ratio	t-ratio	t-ratio	t-ratio
NICs	.002	-.039	.085	.004
	.002	.012	.089	.003
	1.092	-2.860	.964	1.569
SIG	.001	-.001	.0008	-.00002
	.0003	.001	.0057	.0007
	1.736	-1.359	.135	-.023
KOR	.0002	-.002	.021	.0007*
	.0008	.004	.022	.0003
	.224	-.610	.981	2.076
HK	-.0003	-.006	-.035	.006
	.0008	.004	.031	.007
	-.426	-1.562	-1.134	.933
TAW	.001	-.009	-.005	-.0003
	.001	.005	.018	.001
	1.077	-1.783	-.254	-.313

**Significantly different from 0.00 at .05 level.

Table 5.13: Coefficient Estimates for the Mercantilist Equations for
Regional Aggregates at Commodity Level

NIC	TD1	CF	GE	USTA
	b_{i5}	b_{i6}	b_{i7}	b_{i8}
	S.E.	S.E.	S.E.	S.E.
	t-ratio	t-ratio	t-ratio	t-ratio
L1	-0.000	-0.008	0.028	0.001
	0.004	0.003	0.024	0.001
	-0.103	-2.492	1.167	0.975
L2	0.068	0.017	0.049	0.002
	0.065	0.012	0.083	0.003
	1.049	1.505	0.586	0.636
L3	0.016	0.003	0.074	-0.003
	0.020	0.011	0.073	0.002
	0.804	0.324	1.009	-1.110
L4	0.016	-0.002	-0.181	0.040**
	0.012	0.056	0.414	0.013
	1.333	-0.032	-0.438	3.048
L5	0.051	-0.028	-0.212	0.017
	0.067	0.047	0.280	0.010
	0.749	-0.598	-0.759	1.596
L6	0.034	-0.019	-0.025	-0.007
	0.025	0.020	0.144	0.005
	1.377	-0.952	-0.175	-1.445

**Significantly different from 0.00 at .05 level.

The results of the adjusted estimations suggest several interesting points concerning the individual models and their theoretical determinants of import penetration. Among the individual models, the interdependence model which isolates comparative advantage as the major cause of import penetration consistently predicted the highest percentages of estimates with the correct signs. But none of the estimates for comparative advantage is statistically significant. For the individual determinants, the dollar exchange rate and the U.S. GNP growth rate have the highest predictive ratios, with a few statistically significant coefficient estimates. The mercantilist model and its determinants (especially trade dispute and the NICs' capital formation) have failed to explain the variations in the NICs' import penetration into the United States.

Table 5.14 summarizes the results of the adjusted estimations in terms of rank-orderings of the individual models (based on their predictive performances) and lists the variables with the highest predictive ratios for the regional, national and commodity level of analysis.

Table 5.14: A Comparative Evaluation of Individual Models for Their Predictive Performance at Various Types of Analyses**

Type of Analysis	Ranking of Model	Key Variables
Overall	INT > DEP > MER	GNP(62.9%)
Regional	INT > DEP > MER	CA ER GNP GE TA (100%)
Singapore	DEP > MER > INT	GNP GE (100%)
Korea	MER> DEP > INT	GE TA GNP(100%)
Hong Kong	INT > DEP > MER	CA ER GNP TA (100%)
Taiwan	INT > DEP > MER	CA ER GNP (100%)
Regional-L	INT > MER > DEP	CA GNP (83.3%)
Singapore-L	INT > MER > DEP	CA GNP GE TA (50.0%)
Korea-L	INT > MER > DEP	CA (83.3%)
Hong Kong-L	INT > DEP > MER	UEP (83.3%)
Taiwan-L	INT > MER > DEP	GNP (83.3%)

**The models are rank-ordered based on their percentages of estimated coefficients with correct signs; the listed variables are those with the highest predictive ratios for the given type of analysis.

Based on the presentation and interpretation of the results from the tables and from the summary results displayed in Table 5.14, the following conclusions concerning the Pacific Basin NICs' import penetrations into the United States are presented:

(1) Overall, the interdependence model has the highest explanatory power regarding the NICs' import penetration. The interdependence model which had the worst predictive ratio (28.6 percent of estimates predicted correctly) for the unadjusted OLS estimation has the highest predictive ratio (62.9 percent) for the adjusted estimation. By the same token, the mercantilist model regressed from the best (53.6 percent) to the worst (43.6 percent) after the data adjustment. The dependency model consistently scored the second highest rate for both estimations. This means that, on the whole, the interdependence model explains the most variations concerning the NICs' import penetration. For the individual determinants, however, the U.S. GNP growth rate has the highest predictive ratio (65.7 percent), even outperforming comparative advantage (62.9 percent). Generally speaking, the U.S. macroeconomic condition determines the changes in the Pacific Basin NICs' export performances.

(2) For the aggregated regional level of analysis, on the whole, the interdependence model has the highest explanatory power. Nonetheless, a number of the determinants (including, comparative advantage, dollar exchange rate, GNP growth rate, NICs' government expenditure, and U.S. total assistance) have certain impacts on the NICs' import penetration. Furthermore, the dependency determinants of the dollar exchange rate and GNP growth rate are statistically significant. Minimally, it appears that the NICs' import penetration is a multifarious phenomenon, caused by many-- not just one or two--determinants.

(3) At the national level of analysis, although similar, it is clear that the Pacific Basin NICs' are very much different from one another. The Gang of Four share a common sensitivity to U.S. macroeconomic conditions (e.g., the U.S. GNP growth rate), but this is where the similarity ends. Singapore and Korea's import penetrations into the United States are conditioned by active governmental interventions (e.g., government expenditure), while Hong Kong and Taiwan are affected by their competitive labor costs and dollar exchange rates. These dissimilarities suggest that Singapore and Korea are in the "dependent-mercantilist"

relationship, whereas Hong Kong and Taiwan are in the "Interdependent-dependent" trade relationship with the United States.

(4) For the commodity clusters at the regional level of analysis, once again the interdependence model has the highest explanatory power, followed by the dependency model and the mercantilist model. Among the individual determinants, the comparative advantage and the U.S. GNP growth are tied for the highest predictive rate with 83.3 percent of coefficient estimates predicted correctly. These results suggest that the clusters of commodity from the Pacific Basin NICs into the United States are attributed to their competitive labor costs and improving U.S. macroeconomic conditions.

(5) For the import penetration of the commodity clusters at the national level of analysis, the interdependence model (for all four NICs) has the highest explanatory power. However, each NIC's commodity penetration is caused by a number of the different theoretical determinants. Singapore's commodity clusters are affected by its comparative advantage, the U.S. GNP growth rate, the government expenditure, and the U.S. total assistance. For Korea the single most important determinant is its lower labor cost; for Hong Kong, the major determinant is the U.S. unemployment rate; and for Taiwan, it is the U.S. GNP growth rate. On the average, the Pacific Basin NICs import penetrations at the commodity clusters are determined by the labor costs, the U.S. GNP growth rate and the NIC's governmental expenditure. In sum, the results appear to confirm the notion that the Pacific Basin NICs' commodity penetration is indeed a multifarious event.

Comparative Analysis of Individual and Composite Model
The purpose of running the composite model analysis, as mentioned earlier, is to lay the groundwork for a new theory building and/or theoretical synthesis in international trade relations, especially between the United States and the NICs from the Pacific Basin. With this purpose, the composite model equations were estimated following the results of the visual diagnostics.[5]

Table 5.15 summarizes the results of the composite model analysis.[6] With the exception of the commodity clusters for Singapore, Table 5.15 shows that the interdependence model consistently has the highest explanatory power when all three sets of the trade determinants are pooled together. For the individual determinant of import penetration, comparative advantage in labor cost displays a convincing predictive power throughout the composite analyses. Clearly, the Pacific Basin NICs' lower labor costs have an undeniable impact on their success in penetrating the U.S. market.

At the aggregated regional and national level of analysis, the findings suggest that the NICs' import penetration is a complex event caused by a number of relevant factors beside the lower labor costs. In particular, the NICs' import penetrations are affected by macroeconomic factors of the dollar exchange rate, the U.S. GNP growth rate and the unemployment rate, the NIC's governmental expenditure, and the U.S. total assistance. This result strongly implies that the aggregated sums of the NIC's exports into the U.S. markets are caused by a combination of lower labor cost, the U.S. macroeconomic conditions, and the NIC's export promotion policies.

Table 5.15: A Comparative Evaluation of Individual Models from
Composite Analysis for Their Predictive Performance
at Various Types of Analyses**

Type of Analysis	Ranking of Model	Key Variables
Overall	INT > DEP > MER	CA (62.9%)
Regional	INT > DEP > MER	CA ER UEP GE TA (100%)
Singapore	INT > DEP > MER	CA GNP CF (100%)
Korea	INT > DEP > MER	CA UEP TA (100%)
Hong Kong	INT > DEP > MER	CA ER GNP GE TA (100%)
Taiwan	INT > DEP > MER	CA ER GNP GE TA(100%)
Regional-L	INT----DEP > MER	CA ER GNP UEP GE TA (50.0%)
Singapore-L	MER> DEP >INT	ER TD GE TA (66.7%)
Korea-L	INT > DEP > MER	CA UEP CF (66.7%)
Hong Kong-L	INT > MER > DEP	CA UEP TA (66.7%)
Taiwan-L	INT > DEP > MER	CA GNP UEP (66.7%)

**The models are rank-ordered based on their percentages of estimated coefficients with correct signs; the listed variables are those with the highest predictive ratios for the given type of analysis.

In addition, for the commodity clusters at the regional level of analysis, the interdependence and dependency model are tied with the highest explanatory power. In other words, when the models are pooled together, the individual determinants of comparative advantage, the dollar exchange rate, the U.S. GNP growth and unemployment rate, the NIC's governmental expenditure, and the U.S. total assistance have certain causal impacts on the NICs' import penetration into the U.S.

When the models are pooled together, the results of each individual NIC are more diverse, confirming the results from the individual model analyses that each NIC's commodity penetration is driven by a distinct set of rationales. For Singapore, the mercantilist model has the highest power of explanation and its commodity penetration is affected by the dollar exchange rate, the trade dispute, the governmental expenditure, and the U.S. assistance to Singapore. South Korea's commodity penetration is conditioned by its lower labor cost and its domestic capital formation, and the rate of unemployment in the U.S. This finding fits the "interdependent but still dependent" argument of international trade relations. Hong Kong's commodity penetration in the U.S. is stimulated by its lower labor cost, the rate of unemployment in the U.S. and the U.S. total assistance. This seems to suggest that Hong Kong's penetration behavior is less dependent on the United States than originally assumed under the individual model analysis. For Taiwan, the dominant causes of its import penetration are its lower labor cost, GNP growth and unemployment rate of the United States--revealing a similar characteristic with Korea's commodity penetration.

Tables 5.16 and 5.17 present the changes in the signs of the coefficients estimates between the individual and composite analyses. Positive numbers indicate improvements in predicting the expected relationship and negative numbers signify worsened results of the analyses.

According to Tables 5.16 and 5.17, for the overall analyses, the interdependence model shows no improvement over the individual analysis, while the dependency model discloses the most improvement and the mercantilist model shows a slightly worsened result. Among the individual determinants, the U.S. unemployment rate has the highest improvement, while the U.S. GNP growth rate reveals the worst alteration with six additional miss-predictions. For the aggregated regional and national level of analyses, the results of the composite analyses are not significantly different from those of the individual analyses. There are very little or no changes between the individual and composite analyses.

Table 5.16: Changes in the Signs of Coefficient
Estimates between Individual and
Composite Analysis

Type of Analysis	INT	DEP	MER
Overall	0	+4	-1
Regional	0	-1	0
Singapore	+1	0	-1
Korea	+1	0	0
Hong Kong	0	0	0
Taiwan	0	0	0
Regional-L	-2	0	+3
Singapore-L	-1	+3	+3
Korea-L	-1	0	-2
Hong Kong-L	+1	-1	-1
Taiwan-L	+1	-1	-3

Table 5.17: Changes in the Signs of Coefficient Estimates
between Individual and Composite Analysis

Type of Analysis	Variable							
	CA	ER	GNP	UEP	TD	CF	GE	TA
Overall	0	+2	-6	+8	+2	-2	-1	0
Regional	0	0	-1	0	0	0	0	0
Singapore	+1	0	0	0	0	-1	0	0
Korea	+1	0	-1	+1	0	0	0	0
Hong Kong	0	0	0	0	0	0	0	0
Taiwan	0	0	0	0	0	0	0	0
Regional-L	-2	0	-2	+2	+2	+1	0	0
Singapore-L	-1	+2	0	+1	+2	-1	+1	+1
Korea-L	-1	-1	-1	+2	-1	0	-2	+1
Hong Kong-L	+1	0	0	-1	0	0	-1	0
Taiwan-L	+1	+1	-1	+3	-1	-1	+1	-2

Table 5.16 and 5.17 display that the changes are more obvious for the commodity cluster analyses. At the aggregated regional level, the mercantilist model shows the highest improvement while the interdependence model records the worst results. The U.S. unemployment rate and the U.S. trade dispute illuminate the highest improvement over the individual analyses, and at the same time, the U.S. GNP growth rate connotes the worsening expected result.

    For each NIC, the changes are very subtle and distinct. For Singapore, the dependency and mercantilist models are improved over the individual analyses. In fact, the U.S. exchange rate and the U.S. trade dispute display the highest improvement, whereas the labor cost and the domestic capital formation have worsened predictive powers. For Korea, both the interdependence and mercantilist models exhibit worsened estimation results, while the dependency model remains constant. The unemployment rate shows the highest improvement, whereas the NIC's governmental expenditure demonstrates much worsened results. The composite model analysis for Hong Kong shows that the interdependence model has improved slightly and the dependency and mercantilist model have worsened over the individual model analyses.

    In addition, the comparative advantage and government expenditure recorded the best and worst changes, respectively. For Taiwan, the dependency model exhibits the highest improvement, whereas the mercantilist model registers the regressive alteration. In particular, the U.S. unemployment rate denotes the highest improvement and the U.S. total assistance has gotten significantly worse.

    To further the comparative evaluation of the individual and composite model analysis, Tables 5.18 and 5.19 present the percent changes in the coefficient estimates between the analyses. The differences in coefficient estimates between the individual and composite estimations are reported as the absolute differences.[7] These differences would indicate the degree to which the individual models and their determinants are sufficient explanations in dealing with the NIC's import penetration.[8]

    Overall, the dependency model shows the highest average difference (905 percent) between the coefficient estimates of the individual and composite analyses. The interdependence model discloses the second highestdifference (290 percent) and the mercantilist model has the lowest difference (207 percent).

Table 5.18: Absolute Differences of
Coefficient Estimates between
the Individual and Composite
Model (%)

Type of Analysis	INT	DEP	MER
Overall	290	905	207
Regional	89	115	23
Singapore	500	27	50
Korea	800	348	96
Hong Kong	46	53	34
Taiwan	18	49	61

For the aggregated regional and national level of analysis, the results in Table 5.18 reveal that the differences at the regional level are similar to the overall results, the individual NICs, however, display unique differences. The differences are somewhat alike for Singapore and Korea on the one hand, and for Hong Kong and Taiwan on the other hand. Singapore and Korea have the highest deviations from the interdependence model with 500 percent and 800 percent, respectively. The second highest differences are: for Singapore, the mercantilist model with 50 percent, and for Korea, the dependency model with 348 percent. Hong Kong has the highest difference for the dependency model with 53 percent, followed by the interdependence model (46 percent) and the mercantilist model (34 percent). Taiwan shows the highest differences for the mercantilist model with 61 percent, ensued by the dependency model (49 percent) and the interdependence model (18 percent). These differences indicate that at the aggregated national level of analysis: (1) Singapore and Korea present sizable differences, while Hong Kong and Taiwan show much smaller differences, and (2) the magnitude of differences across the models is much higher for Singapore and Korea than Hong Kong and Taiwan.

For each individual determinant, Table 5.19 shows that for the overall and the aggregated regional analysis, the highest differences are reported by the dependency determinants--the U.S. GNP growth, the unemployment, and the dollar exchange rate.

Table 5.19: Absolute Differences of Coefficient Estimates
between the Individual and Composite Model (%)

Type of Analysis	Variable							
	CA	ER	GNP	UEP	TD	CF	GE	TA
Overall	290	624	1151	938	143	328	149	133
Regional	89	98	117	131	50	17	10	25
Singapore	500	17	37	27	0	100	100	0
Korea	800	300	292	452	0	250	33	100
Hong Kong	46	89	15	10	0	0	34	100
Taiwan	18	84	42	22	0	44	200	0

For the aggre gated national analysis, several determinants, including comparative advantage, the dollar exchange rate, the U.S. unemployment rate, the NIC's government expenditure, have shown to deviate from the individual estimates. For Singapore and Korea, the highest deviations are registered by the comparative advantage. For Hong Kong, the U.S. total assistance shows the highest deviation, and the government expenditure unfolds the highest deviation for Taiwan. All four NICs disclosed the least amount of deviation for the trade disputes, and the mercantilist determinants. And consistently, Singapore and Korea produced the more divergent deviations of the coefficient estimates than Hong Kong and Taiwan.

On the whole, the composite model analysis confirms the individual model analyses that the Pacific Basin NICs' import penetrations into the United States are affected by several determinants, including comparative advantage, the U.S. macroeconomic conditions, and the NIC's export policies. Although similar, there are a few differences between the individual and composite model analyses which require further investigation.

First, the composite model analysis shows that Singapore is much more mercantilistic than originally conceived. Clearly, Singapore practices an aggressive export-oriented industrial policy and this becomes more apparent only in the composite model analysis. Second, the U.S. unemployment rate, which was one of the lowest predictive variables for the individual model analysis, became one of the most consistent predictors for the composite model analysis. One possible explanation is that the U.S. unemployment rate is highly correlated with the GNP growth rate and it is only when these two determinants are analyzed along with the third determinant (or even the combinations of several determinants) that we can distinguish its actual impact. Third, the comparative evaluation between the individual and composite models suggests that there are two subgroups within the Pacific Basin NICs: (1) Singapore and Korea, with more mercantilistic tendencies; and (2) Hong Kong and Taiwan, with more dependency overtones. Fourth, throughout the composite model analyses, the most consistent determinant is the NIC's comparative advantage, confirming the conventional wisdom of international trade. Each of the Pacific Basin NICs, however, seems to diverge from this common foundation and has a distinct set of determinants for their success in penetrating the U.S. markets. The analyses demonstrate the fact that the NICs' import penetration can be explained by a number of determinants, including a lower labor cost, an expanding U.S. economy, and a NICs' vigorous export policy. Apparently, it is difficult (perhaps even a mistake) to generalize the Pacific Basin NICs' import penetrations into the United States, without first considering their individual differences.

NOTES

1. The estimates with correct signs are those estimates that correctly predicted the expected directions--either positive or negative--of the causal relationship. The percentages of estimates with the correct signs provide a summary result on "fitness" between the theoretical models and the actual observations.

2. I have estimated 35 equations for each individual model for the total of 105 equations. The four NICs and a regional total together count for 7 equations: one for the aggregated sum for national and regional total plus six for commodity clusters.

3. The variables with both non-stationary series and autocorrelations are: KORPUSL5, TAWPUSL3, KORCAL3, NICER, and HKER.

4. The results of coefficient estimates of commodity level analyses fore each NIC is provided in Appendix C. They are excluded from the text due to their vastness.

5. The visual diagnostics yield the following equations for estimation: 10 adjusted OLS, 16 EGLS, and 0 unadjusted OLS equation. NIC requires 7 EGLS equations; Singapore 7 adjusted OLS equations; Korea requires 6 adjusted OLS and 1 EGLS equation; Hong Kong all 7 EGLS equations, and Taiwan requires 6 adjusted OLS and 1 EGLS equation.

6. The results of coefficient estimates of the composite analyses are provided in Appendix D rather than presented here.

7. The differences are reported as the percent differences in absolute values. They are computed as the absolute differences between the individual and composite coefficient estimate over the individual coefficient estimate: Difference $= \left| (\beta_i - \beta_j)/\beta_i \right|$, where β_i = individual estimate and β_j = composite estimate.

8. The main concern is to determine whether (1) the individual model analyses are theoretically sound in explaining the NIC's trade relations or (2) we need to develop a new theoretical framework to improve our understanding of the phenomenon.

VI

Conclusion

The present study began with the theoretical review and the development of subsequent hypotheses concerned with international trade relations, specifically between the United States and the Pacific Basin NICs. With the completion of the analyses, this chapter provides concluding remarks regarding the major findings and features of the study. First, the findings of the individual and composite model analysis of the interdependence, dependence, and mercantilist perspectives will be reviewed. Then, a broader set of questions concerning the implications of this study and its place within the context of international political economy will be presented. At the end, possible directions of future research to advance our understanding regarding international trade relations will be proposed.

SUGGESTIONS FROM THE ANALYSES

In their book *Beyond Globalism,* Vernon and Spar boldly state that,

> If Americans are confused about where their international economic policies are headed, they have a right to their confusion. The assumptions of the past four decades on which the country's policies once rested have been swept away. The United States is no longer the unchallenged economic leader of the noncommunist world, leading other nations toward an ultimate goal of open global markets. And if that is no longer the objective of the United States, where is the American economy headed?[1]

A part of the confusion is unmistakably connected to the NICs' success in penetrating the U.S. market. An increase in NICs' import penetration into the United States (2.8 percent of the U.S. general imports in 1967 to 11.3 percent in 1985) has coincided with the decline in the U.S. hegemony in the international system.[2]

Based on the findings of the individual and composite model analyses, the following conclusions about the NICs' import penetration into the U.S. market are presented.

Overall, the interdependence model with its emphasis on comparative advantage has the highest explanatory power regarding the NICs' import penetration. The dependency model which is based on macroeconomic conditions, and the mercantilist model which is a policy model, could do no better than a distant second and third, respectively. On the average, the key determinants of the NICs' import penetration are comparative advantage and the U.S. GNP growth rate. That is, a lower labor cost coupled with an improving U.S. macroeconomic condition are the most important causes of import penetration. The study basically confirms the conventional wisdom of international trade that price determines the exchange of commodities.

More importantly, the study also confirms, as pointed out by Harris, that the Pacific Basin NICs are four very different politico-economic systems.[3] Clearly, all four NICs are economically dynamic and are very active trading economies.[4] Although, the NICs share a common sensitivity to external demands and conditions (i.e., the macroeconomic conditions which include the dollar exchange rates and the U.S. GNP growth and unemployment rates), each NIC has a distinct set of determinants, profoundly displaying the divergences among the "Gang of Four."

Singapore is the most mercantilistic of the four NICs. Singapore's import penetration into the United States is conditioned by active governmental interventions, confirming the observation made by Harris that "Singapore is...the predominant state capitalism of mixed economics, replete with consistent Keynesian policies....The state intervenes in almost everything--from the long-term and the strategic, the regulation of currency and the shaping of a future industrial structure."[5] In addition to government interventions, Singapore's success can be directly attributed to external demands, especially that of the U.S. GNP growth rate. The bulk of Singapore's export to the United State is composed of Level 6 commodities (74 percent of its total exports to the United States which consists of: electrical machines (26 percent), radio and television set (15 percent), and office machines (14 percent)), and these commodities are capital and technology intensive commodities. As such, Singapore is very much dependent on international financial and technology systems for its sustained import penetration.

Three remaining NICs (Korea, Hong Kong, and Taiwan) are apparently affected by a similar set of determinants--comparative advantage, the U.S. GNP growth and unemployment rate, and the dollar exchange rate. These three NICs' import penetrations are determined by internally generated cost factors, while at the same time, they are conditioned by external demands and conditions. The import penetrations are affected by their labor costs, but each seems to be conditioned by different external, dependency determinants. Over the years, their import penetrations into the United States have focused on Levels 4 and 6 commodities, these two levels have composed 81 percent of Korea's, 83 percent of Hong Kong's, and 79 percent of Taiwan's export to the United States. Although similar, each of these three NICs has a distinct commodity emphasis. Korea began to focus on high-tech and capital intensive commodities, such as computers, electronic components, and automobiles. Hong Kong has the least diversified export economy, largely relying on a few select commodities (e.g., wearing apparel accounts for 40 percent of its total export to the United States). Taiwan has been more successful in exporting the commodities which require medium processing skills. For instance, among the NICs, it has the highest share of Level 5 commodities, which include metal products (tools), travel goods, and plastic materials.

Among this group, Korea seems the least dependent on external demands and conditions. Although less dependent, Korea's import penetration into the United States is caused primarily by its lower wages for labor: "...if it takes five hours to assemble a computer, it costs just $8 in Korea. In the United States the cost would run between $100 and $200."[6] In this vein, Harris claims that

> ...[The conventional wisdom] explains Korean development as the product of low wages. Since low wages are general in developing countries, South Korea's advantage is limited. Korean wages were not the lowest in the world at the beginning of fast growth,...However, productivity gains more than offset the increase in wages, so that the labor cost of output fell; explaining the productivity gains,...Other factors...which for much of the time reduced the price of exports and made imports relatively expensive.

As a result, Korea's comparative advantage could be clearly expressed.[7]

Hong Kong and Taiwan are the most similar pair among the Four. Both share the common determinants of comparative advantage, dollar exchange rate, and U.S. GNP growth rate. At the same time, Taiwan is closer in terms of its economic tendencies to Korea, while Hong Kong appears to be more sensitive to external demands and conditions. Contextually, Hong Kong and Taiwan have an economic pattern which is dominated by light, labor intensive operations, primarily owned by small and medium companies. Their primary exports are the commodities with a medium level (Levels 4 and 5) of processing, including wearing apparel, footwear, and chemicals. Yet, in a development sense, Hong Kong lacks a state, an agency which endeavors to change the economy to achieve a target pattern of future output. Taiwan is similar to Korea in that both countries face similar domestic and international political climates. Domestically, both states have dominated their economic activities through active state capitalism. Internationally, both Taiwan and Korea have been close allies of the United States and are impelled by a similar context of military insecurities (i.e., mainland China and North Korea).

Figure 6.1 summarizes the findings of the analyses emphasizing the dominant tendencies of the Pacific Basin NICs' import penetration into the United States.

Figure 6.1: The NICs' Tendencies Toward Import Penetration Into the United States

Dependency

	High	Medium	Low
Interdependence	Hong Kong		
		Taiwan	
			Korea
Mercantilist	Singapore		

As Figure 6.1 illustrates, Hong Kong and Singapore are similar in that they are the most sensitive to the dependency determinants. Nonetheless, they differ because Singapore has been more tightly controlled by the state and is thus the most mercantilistic, while Hong Kong lacks state involvement in the conventional sense and is, therefore, the most interdependent or non-political among the NICs.[8] Hong Kong and Taiwan share the similar factors of import penetration, labor cost and external conditions. However, Hong Kong is more dependent on external demand and conditions than is Singapore. Because of its relatively smaller capacity, limited labor force, and fewer natural resources, Hong Kong's share of import penetration among the NICs has steadily decreased over the years. Realizing its limitations, Hong Kong is turning toward more highly specialized "non-trade" service sectors, such as banking and insurance.

Taiwan and Korea are similar in their historical and political backgrounds--that is, both are former Japanese colonies and since their independence were dominated by authoritarian regimes. Consequently, Taiwan and Korea share similar causes of import penetration into the United States. However, the present study suggests that Taiwan is more sensitive to external demands and conditions than is Korea. Taiwan is dominated by a mass of small companies, while Korea is dominated by giant companies (*Jae-Bol*).[9] It is plausible that smaller companies are more sensitive and vulnerable to the changes in the international trade system than are larger corporations. A giant company in Korea, such as Hyundai, is less sensitive and vulnerable to changing external demands and conditions; it is more capable of promoting independently its products during changing international circumstances.[10]

In summary, there are certain similarities and dissimilarities between the Pacific Basin NICs. It is incorrect, even absurd, to generalize about the Pacific Basin NICs as a single group of developing economies. Each NIC is very different from one another. Nevertheless, pairs of the NICs are somewhat similar: Singapore and Hong Kong are the most dependent economies; Hong Kong and Taiwan are somewhat more interdependent; Taiwan and Korea share similar historical and political backgrounds, and, Singapore and Korea exhibit more mercantilistic tendencies.

POLICY IMPLICATIONS OF THE STUDY

For the United States

The present study reveals a number of policy implications for both the United States and the Pacific Basin NICs. As noted by Bergsten, the United States has, in recent years, experienced a rapidly changing international economic situation evidenced by rising budget and trade deficits:

> ...[Bush administration and Congress] will confront a current account deficit that remains well over $100 billion, and that will probably never fall much below $100 billion on the basis of present policies and exchange rates....a United States that is for the first time in modern history the world's largest debtor, with a net foreign debt that could rise to $1 trillion in the early 1990s in the absence of corrective action. They will face growing concern, both at home and abroad, that the United States can no longer compete effectively in the world economy and is losing its leadership role and ability.[11]

Concurrently, Cuomo proclaims that

> America has failed to adjust to the new reality of a global economy, and we are beginning to pay the price. The price of failure will not be just economic; the consequences in the next decade will be more than a slower rate of economic growth or a stagnation in living standards and opportunities. Just as any debtor is at the mercy of its creditors, if the U.S. continues to sink into debt, our foreign creditors will eventually have undue influence over our future and the policies of our elected government.[12]

As noted above, the problem facing the United States is obvious and is critical in many ways. The United States, in order to restore its stability, must plan for a structural reduction in her trade and budget deficits.[13] But questions remain as to what the United States needs to do and how the United States will accomplish those needs.

The present study implies a number of specific recommendations to reduce the U.S. trade deficit. One obvious way is to decrease the import penetration from the NICs. Based on the present analysis, the most consistent cause of the NICs' import penetration into the United States is their relatively low labor costs. It confirms the conventional wisdom that the United States must restore the comparative advantages in its commodity production, either in terms of competitive production costs and/or an increased productivity. In this regard, Cuomo writes that "The trade deficit is perhaps the most outstanding manifestation of the American loss of competitiveness,"[14] and suggests that

> To increase our productivity and produce what we are truly capable of producing: that is the great profit of participation...the success of a collective enterprise--be it a company or a nation--depends on the contribution of the individuals that are part of it. Each of us must be given a chance to participate. Once given that chance, *we must do our share.*[15]

At the same time, the United States must persuade the NICs, especially Singapore and Korea, to reduce those governmental controls over the labor market which have kept labor costs below international market wages. The Korean government in particular has successfully suppressed any expression of discontent aimed at its strict control of labor. The United States would benefit by pressuring Korea and Singapore to allow unionization of the labor forces. Since their industries are dominated by giant companies, employing thousands of laborers, unions would undoubtedly raise wages. The United States would benefit by pressuring Hong Kong and Taiwan to adopt and enforce more rigorous employment regulations and building codes, including health and sanitation standards for their factories, which are mostly of small and medium size. This would raise costs of production in Hong Kong and Taiwan.

Another possible adjustment to reduce the trade deficit is further manipulation of the dollar exchange rate. This strategy, however, is not as convincing as that of building comparative advantage. Cuomo hints at this point by noting that "no single macroeconomic policy, such as a lower value of the dollar, will miraculously solve all the problems."[16] He also argues that "trying to buy competitiveness with a cheap dollar will not work. Instead we have to earn it by producing goods and services that our own people and the rest of the world want [at the prices that they are willing to pay]."[17]

The dollar exchange rate does have an impact in reducing the U.S. trade deficit under certain conditions. The United States must maintain a lower value of the dollar against the NICs' currencies while coordinating this effort with other relevant policies. More importantly, the United States must constantly strive to keep the value of the dollar from being too low, because if the dollar value becomes too low, it will prompt various negative consequences: inflation, a decline in the U.S. living standards, a global recession, and (possibly) an international market crash.

The above points and arguments imply that, in order to reduce its trade deficit, the U.S. government must be aggressively involved in the process of international trade. In particular, the U.S. government must be an active partner in facilitating a competitive edge in the international market through more energetic export financing, more incentive structures, and continued technological innovations.[18] Minimally, the United States must face the international reality that it is no longer the hegemonic actor: it is the strongest single nation (or the strongest among the equals), no longer dominating the system, but still with enough veto power to block the initiatives of others.

For the Pacific Basin NICs

Aside from reducing the NICs' import penetration, the United States seeks to reduce its trade deficits by increasing its export shares to the NICs. Recent evidence suggests that the U.S. government is pressuring the Pacific Basin NICs to open the various markets for U.S. goods and services. In addition to the argument of reciprocity, United States has insisted on the theme that

> A hard landing of the American economy would have enormous effects on other countries, most of which are far more dependent on international trade and international financial stability than is the United States. Their major market would shrink abruptly. Their own interest rates would be driven up by the rise in American interest rates. Renewed global inflation would threaten,...The bulk of the American adjustment must therefore be targeted on the small number of countries that are running surpluses: Japan, Germany and a few smaller European countries, and the Asian NICs (notably Taiwan and Korea).[19]

Simply put, the Pacific Basin NICs will be forced to accept the solution proposed by the United States. The NICs will be forced to open their closed markets to U.S. commodities, and they must do this soon. Examples include the United States' push for the opening of various service sectors (e.g., banking, insurance, and stocks) from the NICs and urging the NICs to open agricultural markets (e.g., cigarette, wine, and fruit). The NICs should and must open their markets to U.S. goods and services, when their domestic industrial producers are sufficiently competitive in the international market. However, the United States must not be too hasty in its demands, or it may produce negative effects on both the United States and the NICs. As shown in the analyses, the NICs' import penetration tends to increase when the United States experiences a higher rate of overall growth. Quite clearly, the NICs should not bite the hands that feed them. By the same token, the analyses imply that U.S. goods and services are more likely to penetrate the NICs' market when they experience higher rates of growth. Specifically, the United States would benefit by avoiding any overt protectionist policies toward the Pacific Basin NICs. They would need to sustain a higher rate of overall growth to facilitate an increase in their consumption of U.S. goods and services.

In addition, the solution proposed by the United States would compel the NICs to diversify their export markets. Up to now, the United States has been viewed as the prime export market; but, from now on, the NICs must actively look to non-American markets to maintain their export-led economies. Cuomo points out that

> Agreements are needed to shift imports away from the U.S. to those countries which maintain large trade surpluses. Today, the NICs and developing countries are where Japan was decades ago, and once again the U.S. must work to see that Europe--and Japan--accept more exports from these dynamic young economies. Currently, many developing countries have their eyes fixed almost exclusively on the American markets, and work with the other advanced countries to ensure that they will accept more exports from the Third World.[20]

Such an attempt made by the United States to diffuse the NICs' export markets could be viewed as a part of burden sharing. Japan, Europe, and the NICs must share relatively equal responsibilities in maintaining the international system by providing their fair share of global military security, and by being more actively involved in providing economic assistance. Along the way, the Pacific Basin NICs may be forced to divert their surplus from U.S. trade to assist other Third World countries in the region (e.g., the Southeast Asian countries).

THEORETICAL IMPLICATION OF THE STUDY

The present study empirically tested the models of import penetration based on the causal factors suggested by the three major theoretical perspectives. The interdependence model, which emphasizes comparative advantage among producers, is a microeconomic explanation of international trade. The dependency model focuses on the macroeconomic determinants of international trade, including U.S. dollar exchange, U.S. GNP growth, and U.S. unemployment rates. The mercantilist model, as a policy explanation, is concerned with the self-centered policies of trading nations as represented by trade disputes, NICs' domestic capital formation and government expenditures, and U.S. economic and military assistance to the NICs.

These models were tested on three levels of analysis: (1) a regional level using an aggregate sum for all the NICs; (2) a national level using a national total for each NIC; and, (3) a commodity level using the total for each of six clusters of commodities.

In terms of theoretical clarity, the interdependence model is the most explicit of the three models, suggesting that the hypothesized relationship exists at the commodity level of analysis. The dependency and mercantilist models, on the other hand, are not explicitly concerned with the micro or commodity level of analysis.

The dependency and mercantilist models place emphasis on the aggregate or macro level of analysis. These models do not, however, preclude the possibility that relationship might exist at the commodity level of analysis. The results of the analyses indicate that the dependency and mercantilist focus on macro relationships is due more to the lack of attention to the micro level of analysis than to the nature of their theoretical frameworks (i.e., this is not an essential neglect, these models are just more concerned with the holistic approach). Throughout the analyses, the dependency and mercantilist determinants registered about equal percentages of estimates with the correct signs for the macro and micro levels of analysis. These results suggest no inherent limitations in the dependency and mercantilist models in dealing with the micro level of analysis.

Overall, It seems that each individual model, to somewhat varying extent, is a necessary, but not sufficient condition for import penetration from the NICs into the United States. To explore the theoretical implications, the interdependence model had the highest predictive ratio

(63 percent), followed by the dependency model (48 percent) and the mercantilist model (44 percent). Among the individual determinants, the U.S. GNP growth rate and comparative advantage had the highest predictive ratios with 66 and 63 percents of estimates with the correct signs. A similar result was found at the commodity level of analysis--the interdependence model had the highest explanatory power, followed by the dependency and mercantilist models. These results from both the overall and the commodity level of analysis confirm the argument that import penetrations from the Pacific Basin NICs into the United States can be attributed to their competitive labor costs and improving U.S. macroeconomic conditions. The study supports the viewpoint that trade relations should be viewed from labor/production costs within a broader, macroeconomic setting.

Although comparative advantage had the highest explanatory power, at the aggregated regional and national levels of analysis, the other determinants such as dollar exchange rate, GNP growth rate, NICs' government expenditure, and U.S. total assistance had certain impacts on the NICs' import penetration. As mentioned earlier, it is clear that the Pacific Basin NICs are very much different from one another. The Gang of Four shares a common sensitivity to U.S. macroeconomic conditions (e.g., the U.S. GNP growth rate), but this is where the similarity ends. Singapore and Korea's import penetrations into the United States are conditioned by active governmental interventions as indicated by a higher government expenditure, while Hong Kong and Taiwan are affected by their competitive labor costs and dollar exchange rates. Minimally, it appears that the NICs' import penetration is a complex event, caused by a number of (not just one or two) determinants.

Theoretically, the present study suggests that no single model has the explanatory power to account for all the variations of the Pacific Basin NICs' import penetration into the United States. The composite model analysis indicated that the individual model approach to analysis yields a somewhat insufficient rationale in explaining the phenomena of import penetration. Based on the findings and suggestions of the various analyses, the following recommendations which may serve as a basis for development of a new theory and/or theoretical synthesis of international trade relations are offered:

First, international trade relations should be thought of as a complex event. More precisely, in addition to the single equation model, some alternative models of international trade need to be developed (e.g., the simultaneous model and the dynamic model). It may be that a single equation approach (i.e., individual model analysis) is an inadequate way of analyzing international trade relations. It is plausible to conceptualize trade relations as a simultaneous event caused by commodity penetration and protectionist trade policy (see Appendix B). Although some theorists have argued that import penetration and protectionist trade policy are essentially the same event, these events may be individual and independent outcomes; if so, they may be considered to be simultaneous events. In other words, there may exist a feedback effect between import penetration on the one side and protectionism on the other side--as import penetration increases, the demand for protectionism increases, at the same time.

For example, a simultaneous model of import penetration can be formalized as follows:

$$Y_1 = r_{12}Y_2 + B_{11}X_1 + B_{12}X_2 + B_{13}X_3 + B_{15}X_5 + U_{1t} \qquad (6.1)$$
$$Y_2 = r_{21}Y1 + B_{22}X_2 + B_{23}X_3 + B_{24}X_4 + B_{25}X_5 + U_{2t} \qquad (6.2)$$

where Y_1 = import penetration
               Y_2 = trade dispute
               X_1 = comparative advantage
               X_2 = exchange rate
               X_3 = GNP growth rate
               X_4 = U.S. foreign aid
               X_5 = NIC's export policy
               U_ts = error term

This simultaneous model may provide a new insight in dealing with international trade and advance our understanding regarding the NICs' import penetration into the United States to a single, linear equation approach.

Second, it is necessary to synthesize the individual explanations to possibly provide a more plausible account of current circumstances. The analyses have suggested that the interdependence model, with its emphasis on comparative advantage, has the highest explanatory power regarding the NICs' import penetration. Although the dependency model which is based on macroeconomic conditions, and the mercantilist model, a policy model, could do no better than a distant second and third, it is possible to develop: (a) the interdependence-dependency model, and (b) the interdependence-mercantilist model.

Because the key determinants of the NICs' import penetration are comparative advantage and the U.S. GNP growth rate, it may be possible to synthesize the microeconomic and macroeconomic determinants of international trade into a single model to account for the variations of the Pacific Basin NICs' import penetration into the United States. This would be an integrative economic model which might consist of comparative advantage, dollar exchange rate, and U.S. GNP growth rate.[21]

The interdependence and mercantilist determinants could be combined to address the relationship between the NICs' import penetration and comparative advantages, while controlling for the NICs' mercantilistic policies. The present study has indicated that a lower labor cost is the most important cause of import penetration. The Heckscher-Ohlin comparative advantage argument is based on naturally endowed production factors, and assumes that flows of commodities are carried out in purely economic, market conditions--completely divorced from political regulations or interventions. This is a questionable assumption and it is credible to ask whether NICs' lower labor costs are naturally endowed factors or result from governmental controls.

As such, this second synthesized model would consist of comparative advantage and the NICs' domestic policy toward labor forces. If the NICs' lower labor cost is a naturally endowed factor, then we would expect to find a strong relationship between comparative advantage and import penetration while holding the NICs' labor policy constant. And if not, we would expect to find a weak or significantly reduced relationship when the NICs' labor policy is introduced into the analysis. In this way, this synthesis model may confirm or disconfirm the conventional wisdom of international trade that commodity penetration is simply determined by naturally endowed production factors, as defined by a lower labor cost.

Third, the following factors and conditions need to be considered in developing a new theory of international trade relations: (a) There is a need to specify and enunciate the historical conditions and specific rules, domestic and interstate, which govern the international trade system. It is necessary to identify the cultural differences and ethical factors of international trade; (b) More attention should be paid to the political side of the international trade system--that is, economic relations should be viewed as political activities, or at least, state as being an important actor; and,(c) More attention should be paid to the role played by the government and other domestic interests in contributing to the internal dynamics of the international trade system.

CAVEATS AND PROSPECTS

It is clear from the analysis and from the discussion of the study that the Pacific Basin NICs are important participants in international trade. In a final note, the plausibility of the present study's external validity and some of its shortcomings in terms of construct validity will be discussed as well as possible directions of future research.

The external validity of the present study concerns replicability over other places and times. Is it plausible that the current study can be replicated over other sets of countries for some other time periods? It is very likely that this question can be answered in the affirmative. For instance, the study could be duplicated over the Southeast Asian NICs (ASEAN, Association of South-Eastern Asian Nations) and the Latin American NICs, such as Brazil, Argentina, and Mexico. In this regard, Cuomo affirmed that "The `Four Tigers' of East Asia--Korea, Taiwan, Singapore, and Hong Kong--got most of the publicity, but industrialization was becoming a brand phenomenon, and countries like Thailand, Malaysia, Bangladesh, and Pakistan were beginning to figure in U.S. trade statistics."[22] Furthermore, a similar study could be undertaken for the Central and Latin American NICs to see if a similar set of determinants can be attributed as causes of their import penetration. In addition, for replicability over time, a similar analysis can be undertaken for longer or shorter periods of time for any given set of the NICs, or for any group of countries.

Aside from the present study's replicability, there are several methodological and theoretical issues which should be explored. There are certain questions concerning construct validities of the variables employed in the present study. That is, there are certain questions concerning the fit between the theoretical constructs and the precise indicators. The problems associated with construct validities may be the most severe for the mercantilist determinants of import penetrations. The present study utilizes the macro, broad measures of the NICs' export policies to represent their mercantilist interests in trade relations. For instance, the present study employs U.S. total economic and military assistance to capture American security interests bestowed on a particular NIC. Although this indicator does not capture the U.S. economic interests in those NICs, it was not possible to reconstruct more reliable data. The data which summarizes U.S. economic and financial interest in the NICs were impossible to obtain on an annual basis--Hong Kong reports the percentage of the U.S. direct investment, but other NICs, especially Korea and Taiwan, do not.

Furthermore, for the NICs' mercantilistic policy, the present study employed the NICs' domestic capital formation and government expenditure rather than other, more representative, indicators. Governmental assistance data for export productions are usually confidential and are very difficult to obtain. Because of the unavailability of this data, export policies of NICs were approximated from the rates of domestic capital formation and domestic governmental expenditure. In addition, there may be a similar problem of construct validities for the dependency determinants--whether these variables actually represent the theoretical constructs of the dependency perspective, especially for dollar exchange rates and U.S. GNP growth rate.

With respect to the merits of the present study, one of the major contributions is its presentation of several, new variables of international trade. In particular, the present study introduces a new approach in conceptualizing trade disputes and comparative advantage. Import penetration is categorized into six commodity clusters to allow a micro level of analysis, which is rarely done in cross-national analysis. Moreover, the data set is inspected and adjusted for autocorrelation and trend prior to estimation procedures. By introducing and undertaking these issues, the present study has explored some new possibilities in analyzing international trade. It is obvious that greater attention should be directed toward the formulation of new concepts and methodologies in the study of international trade. Attention needs to be focused on developing new variables of international trade. Examples are: a variable that describes governmental control over export production and labor wage, a variable that characterizes a country's dependence on the international system, and a variable that captures domestic demand for protectionism.

By following these caveats, prospects, and theoretical implications, a continuous process of thinking and rethinking international trade relations in order to bring about an egalitarian and non-dominated discourse in the realm of international political economy becomes possible and attainable.

NOTES

1. Raymond Vernon and Debora Spar, *Beyond Globalism: Remaking American Foreign Economic Policy* (New York: Free Press, 1989), p. 1.
2. Considerable attention has been focused on this increasingly relevant theme. See Robert O. Keohane, *After Hegemony: Cooperation and Discord in the World Political Economy* (Princeton: Princeton University Press, 1984); C. Fred Bergsten, *America in the World Economy: A Strategy for the 1990s* (Washington, DC: Institute for International Economics, 1988a); C. Fred Bergsten,"US International Macroeconomic Policy," in *Economic Relations between the United States and Korea: Conflict or Cooperation*, ed. Thomas Bayard and Soo-Gil Young (Washington, DC: Institute for International Economics, 1988b); *Cuomo Commission Report*, Cuomo Commission on Trade and Competitiveness, (New York: Touchstone Book, 1988); and Vernon and Spar.
3. See Niegel Harris, *The End of the Third World: Newly Industrializing Countries and the Decline of an Ideology* (New York: Penguin Books, 1986), p. 68. Indeed policies pursued by the Pacific Basin NICs were frequently different, as were their attitudes, endowments, histories, and sizes of economy.
4. Ibid., p. 60-61.
5. Ibid., p. 60.
6. Russell Glitman,"Korean Firms Chalk Up Surprising Sales Success In the U.S. Micro Market," *PC Week* 9 (September 1986), p. 181.
7. Harris, p. 43.
8. Harris notes that Hong Kong has no economic strategy nor long-term plan, no great state investment wielded as instruments of public ambitions.
9. As pointed out by Glitman, p. 181, "The PCS leave the $500 million plant on trucks made by Hyundai and are loaded onto container ships built and owned by Hyundai. Their destination: the United States."
10. Sensitivity is defined as a degree of responsiveness within a policy framework, and vulnerability is defined as an actor's liability to suffer costs imposed by external events after policies have been altered. See Robert O. Keohane and Joseph S. Nye, *Power and Interdependence: World Politics in Transition*, 2nd ed., (Boston: Little, Brown and Company, 1989), p. 11-19.

11. Bergsten, *America in World*, p. 1.

12. Cuomo, p. 1.

13. The figures for U.S. budget and trade deficits are presented in Appendix E.

14. Cuomo, p. 12.

15. Ibid., p. 183.

16. Ibid., p. 21.

17. Ibid., p. 96-97.

18. This could be promoted by assisting the Export-Import Bank of the United States (Eximbank) in financing small and medium size U.S. manufacturers, who cannot finance sales with their own limited resources, are trying to get into the export game, and need commercial lending to support their deals. See Bruce Stokes, "A Thorny Agenda Facing Eximbank," *National Journal* 45 (1988): 2800-01.

19. Bergsten, *America in World*, p. 13.

20. Cuomo, p. 80.

21. Although this may appear to be an overtly inductive approach, theoretically speaking, the dependency model of trade relations shares much common ground with the interdependency model. These models are more complimentary than competitive when comparing how each explains import penetrations. Both hold that trade relations are motivated by economic factors and are fueled by the notions of profitability.

22. Cuomo, p. 58.

Appendix A

UNITED STATES IMPORTS BY LEVELS OF PROCESSING

U.S. imports are coded by the Standard International Trade Classification (SITC) and my categorization is based on the two-digit SITC commodities. There are total of 62 two-digit SITCs and each level of processing consisted of:

Level 1--17 SITCs,
Level 2--10 SITCs,
Level 3--4 SITCs,
Level 4--13 SITCs,
Level 5--7 SITCs, and
Level 6--11 SITCs.

Level	SITC	Commodity
1	00	animal (live)
	02	dairy and egg
	03	fish
	04	cereals
	05	vegetable and fruit
	07	coffee and tea
	08	feeding stuff
	12	tobacco
	21	hide, skin and furskin
	22	oil seed and nuts
	26	textile fiber

	27	crude fertilizer
	28	metal ores
	29	animal, vegetable material
	32	coal
	33	petroleum
	34	natural gas
2	06	sugar and syrups
	23	rubber (crude)
	24	wood (log, lumber)
	25	pulp
	41	animal oil and fat
	42	vegetable oil and fat
	43	processed animal oil
	61	leather
3	11	beverage (wine, beer, spirit)
	65	textile yarn, fabric, tile
	66	nonmetallic mineral (lime, glass)
	68	nonferrous metal (silver, copper)
4	51	organic chemical
	52	inorganic chemical
	53	dyeing, tanning material
	55	perfume material
	56	fertilizer
	59	chemical product (pesticide)
	63	wood manufactured
	64	paper and paper manufactured
	67	iron, steel (plate, pipe, pig iron)
	81	light fixture
	82	furniture
	84	wearing apparel
	85	footwear
5	54	medical and pharmaceutical product
	57	explosive and pyrotechnical product
	58	synthetic and plastic material
	62	tire and tube
	69	metal product (structure, nail, tool)
	83	travel good
	88	photographic apparatus
6	71	power generating machine
	72	electrical machine

73	metal working machine
74	general industrial machine
75	office machine (typewriter, calculator)
76	telecommunication machine (TV, radio)
77	electrical machine (circuit, transistor)
78	road vehicle
79	other transportation equipment
87	scientific and professional instrument
89	other manufactured product (piano)

Appendix B

A SIMULTANEOUS MODEL OF INTERNATIONAL TRADE

As mentioned earlier, there seems to be a gap between the economic analyses which focus on import penetration and the political analyses which highlight protectionism. Although most are unaware, some theorists have argued that because import penetration and protectionism are essentially the same event (i.e., different sides of same coin) they need not or cannot be view separately. However, my contention is that they must be treated as individual outcomes. If this is the case, these two events are indeed simultaneous. Consequently, it is only reasonable to assume that there is a feedback effect between import penetration on the one side and protectionism on the other side. As import penetration increases the demand for protectionism, at the same time, increases. A simultaneous model of import penetration can be formalized as follows:

$$Y_1 = r_{12}Y_2 + B_{11}X_1 + B_{12}X_2 + B_{13}X_3 + B_{15}X_5 + U_{1t} \qquad \text{(B.1)}$$
$$Y_2 = r_{21}Y1 + B_{22}X_2 + B_{23}X_3 + B_{24}X_4 + B_{25}X_5 + U_{2t} \qquad \text{(B.2)}$$

where Y_1 = import penetration
Y_2 = trade dispute
X_1 = comparative advantage
X_2 = exchange rate
X_3 = GNP growth rate
X_4 = U.S. foreign aid
X_5 = NIC's export policy
U_ts = error term

For the simultaneous model, we must examine the questions concerning identification and estimation. Identification is a question of how much prior information is needed in specifying a model. It is a theoretical question as to whether a different form of the structural model could have generated the observed relationship. Specifically, for a simultaneous model to be identified, two conditions must be fulfilled: the order condition, which is a necessary condition and the rank condition which is a necessary and sufficient condition for identification.

The order condition requires that the number of excluded predetermined variables must be at least as great as the number of endogenous variables minus one. For the equations (4.1) and (4.2), we have excluded *one* predetermined variable (X_4 and X_1, respectively) and have included *two* endogenous variables (Y_1 and Y_2). For the rank condition, the equations (B.1) and (B.2) have the rank of *one* while both equations include two endogenous variables. Therefore, both equations are said to be "just identified," fulfilling the requirements of the order and rank conditions.

For identified simultaneous models, estimation techniques fall into two classes: single equation technique and system wide technique. The coefficients can be estimated through the single equation techniques such as two stage least squares and through system wide techniques as LISREL, a full information system. An actual technique selected for the analysis hinges on the availability of data and is subjected to the budget constraints.

Appendix C

RESULTS OF ESTIMATES FROM THE INDIVIDUAL MODELS AT COMMODITY LEVEL OF ANALYSIS

Table C.1: Coefficient Estimates for the Interdependence Equations at the Commodity Level for Inividual NIC

	SIG	KOR	HK	TAW
	b_{i1}	b_{i1}	b_{i1}	b_{i1}
	S.E.	S.E.	S.E.	S.E.
	T-Ratio	T-Ratio	T-Ratio	T-
CAL1	.022	.002	.018	.104
	.146	.041	.006	.110
	.153	.485	2.936	.945
CAL2	-.167	-.007	-.002	-
	.197	.005	.001	.063
	-.847	-.159	-1.604	-2.227
CAL3	.101	-.050	.005	.027
	.064	.063	.038	.034
	1.574	-.793	.128	.800
CAL4	.066	-.266	-.015	-
	.167	.271	.143	.175
	.395	-.982	-.107	-2.023
CAL5	-.005	-.012	-.080	.051
	.050	.024	.073	.069
	-.094	-.492	-1.097	.745
CAL6	-.638*	-.384*	.142	-.378
	.335	.218	.162	.422
	-1.904	-1.764	.880	-.218

*Significantly different from 0.00 at .10 level.
**Significantly different from 0.00 at .05 level.

Table C.2: Coefficient Estimates of the Dependence Equations at the Commodity Level for Singapore

	ER	GNP	UEP
	b_{12}	b_{13}	b_{14}
SIG	S.E.	S.E.	S.E.
	T-Ratio	T-Ratio	T-Ratio
L1	-0.119	-0.143	0.765
	0.244	0.929	1.845
	-0.487	-0.153	0.414
L2	-0.088	-3.317	-7.189**
	0.335	1.275	2.533
	-0.262	-2.601	-2.839
L3	0.047	0.197	0.395
	0.078	0.295	0.587
	0.608	0.668	0.673
L4	-0.272	-0.582	-2.228
	0.208	0.792	1.573
	-1.307	-0.734	-1.417
L5	-0.039	0.154	0.001
	0.064	0.245	0.486
	-0.613	0.629	0.001
L6	0.604	3.895**	8.555
	0.477	1.815	3.604
	1.267	2.146	2.374

** Significantly different from 0.00 at .05 level.

Table C.3: Coefficient Estimates of the Dependence Equations at the Commodity Level for Korea*

KOR	ER b_{i2} S.E. T-Ratio	GNP b_{i3} S.E. T-Ratio	UEP b_{i4} S.E. T-Ratio
L1	-0.104	-0.414	-0.497
	0.033	0.192	0.367
	-3.169	-2.160	-1.356
L2	-0.004	0.014	0.051
	0.004	0.024	0.046
	-0.922	0.570	1.118
L3	0.058	0.080	0.087
	0.043	0.249	0.476
	1.364	0.321	0.182
L4	0.008	-0.006	0.261
	0.236	1.374	2.627
	0.036	-0.005	0.099
L5	0.014	0.214	0.191
	0.025	0.148	0.283
	0.574	1.448	0.674
L6	-0.127	-0.551	-1.274
	0.187	1.093	2.088
	-0.676	-0.504	-0.610

*All coefficients not significantly different from 0.00 at .05 level.

Table C.4: Coefficient Estimates of the Dependence Equations at the Commodity Level for Hong Kong*

HK	ER b_{i2} S.E. T-Ratio	GNP b_{i3} S.E. T-Ratio	UEP b_{i4} S.E. T-Ratio
L1	-0.011 0.004 -3.028	-0.039 0.029 -1.344	-0.74 0.060 -1.239
L2	0.001 0.001 1.265	-0.011 0.007 -1.617	-0.020 0.014 -1.472
L3	-0.015 0.032 -0.479	-0.030 0.218 -0.138	-0.431 0.444 -0.971
L4	-0.011 0.094 -0.120	0.343 0.702 .0488	1.319 1.432 0.921
L5	-0.007 0.055 -0.123	0.185 0.416 0.445	-0.149 0.849 -0.175
L6	0.051 0.102 0.505	-0.394 0.796 -0.494	-0.529 1.622 -0.326

*All coefficients not significantly different from 0.00 at .05 level.

Table C.5: Coefficient Estimates of the Dependence Equations at the
Commodity Level for Taiwan*

TAW	ER b_{i2} S.E. T-Ratio	GNP b_{i3} S.E. T-Ratio	UEP b_{i4} S.E. T-Ratio
L1	0.018	-0.086	0.098
	0.284	0.471	0.930
	0.064	-0.182	0.105
L2	-0.186	0.182	1.047
	0.189	0.314	0.620
	-0.985	0.581	1.690
L3	-0.073	0.077	0.187
	0.075	0.105	0.200
	-0.971	0.733	0.938
L4	-0.039	0.090	1.096
	0.445	0.739	1.459
	-0.088	0.122	0.751
L5	-0.149	0.114	0.012
	0.176	0.292	0.576
	-0.847	0.390	0.022
L6	0.456	0.121	-1.734
	0.478	0.793	1.565
	0.954	0.153	-1.108

*All coefficients not significantly different from 0.00 at
.05 level.

Table C.6: Coefficient Estimates of the Mercantilist Equations at the
Commodity Level for Singapore

SIG	TD1 b_{i1} S.E. T-Ratio	CF b_{i1} S.E. T-Ratio	GE b_{i1} S.E. T-Ratio	USTA b_{i1} S.E. T-Ratio
L1	-0.064	-0.062	-0.575	-0.058
	0.106	0.045	0.267	0.032
	-0.597	-1.381	-2.152	-1.840
L2	0.192	-0.072	-0.469	-0.007
	1.110	0.096	0.570	0.075
	0.173	-0.756	-0.823	-0.090
L3	-0.062	0.027	0.104	-0.007
	1.110	0.096	0.570	0.075
	0.173	-0.756	-0.823	-0.090
L4	0.035	-0.009	-0.090	0.035
	0.018	0.004	0.263	0.031
	1.902	-2.234	-0.342	1.101
L5	0.035	-0.010	0.088	0.013
	0.046	0.015	0.089	0.011
	0.766	-0.659	0.985	1.140
L6	0.333	0.221**	0.935	0.024
	0.206	0.084	0.488	0.059
	1.614	2.630	1.917	0.409

**Significantly different from 0.00 at .05 level.

Table C.7: Coefficient Estimates of the Mercantilist Equations at the Commodity Level for Korea

KOR	TD1 b_{i1} S.E. T-Ratio	CF b_{i1} S.E. T-Ratio	GE b_{i1} S.E. T-Ratio	USTA b_{i1} S.E. T-Ratio
L1	0.009	0.049	0.072	0.001
	0.030	0.020.	0.111	0.002
	0.301	2.427	0.348	0.587
L2	-0.001	0.000	-0.011	0.000
	0.014	0.002	0.013	0.000
	-0.040	0.002	-0.878	1.196
L3	0.025	-0.013	0.008	-0.002
	0.066	0.030	0.134	0.002
	0.383	-0.449	0.063	-0.821
L4	-0.010	-0.086	-0.379	-0.002
	0.033	0.130	0.724	0.011
	-0.320	-0.663	-0.524	-0.157
L5	0.018	0.014	0.131	-0.001
	0.021	0.014	0.070	0.001
	0.858	0.973	1.866	-0.700
L6	0.153	0.202**	0.290	-0.002
	0.156	0.103	0.546	0.008
	0.981	1.963	0.530	-0.239

**Significantly different from 0.00 at .05 level.

Table C.8: Coefficient Estimates of the Mercantilist Equations at the Commodity Level for Hong Kong*

	TD1	CF	GE	USTA
	b_{i1}	b_{i1}	b_{i1}	b_{i1}
SIG	S.E.	S.E.	S.E.	S.E.
	T-Ratio	T-Ratio	T-Ratio	T-Ratio
L1	-0.003	0.001	-0.003	0.002
	0.005	0.003	0.028	0.006
	-0.490	0.405	-0.106	0.304
L2	0.007	-0.001	-0.004	0.001
	0.004	0.001	0.005	0.001
	1.0579	-1.022	-0.784	0.859
L3	0.079	0.006	0.135	-0.012
	0.045	0.017	0.155	0.034
	1.767	0.340	0.872	-0.358
L4	-0.006	-0.036	-0.557	0.140
	0.018	0.061	0.521	0.114
	-0.353	-0.590	-1.069	1.228
L5	0.090	0.028	0.246	-0.061
	0.067	0.036	0.302	0.066
	1.333	0.772	0.815	-0.922
L6	0.099	-0.009	0.023	-0.000
	0.137	0.076	0.638	0.149
	0.718	-0.115	0.036	-0.001

*All coefficients not significantly different from 0.00 at .05 level

Table C.9: Coefficient Estimates of the Mercantilist Equations at the Commodity Level for Taiwan

SIG	TD1 b_{il} S.E. T-Ratio	CF b_{il} S.E. T-Ratio	GE b_{il} S.E. T-Ratio	USTA b_{il} S.E. T-Ratio
L1	0.077	-0.004	-0.087	-0.003
	0.074	0.047	0.158	0.009
	1.038	-0.088	-0.549	-0.360
L2	-0.422**	0.049	0.182**	-0.000
	0.131	0.022	0.073	0.004
	-3.234	2.198	2.482	-0.125
L3	0.021	-0.008	0.008	0.002
	0.037	0.014	0.058	0.002
	0.552	-0.570	0.139	0.827
L4	-0.008	0.069	0.332	-0.004
	0.021	0.079	0.252	0.015
	-0.356	0.878	1.316	-0.250
L5	0.013	-0.033	-0.016	0.004
	0.050	0.032	0.102	0.005
	0.249	-1.018	-0.159	0.765
L6	-0.039	-0.097	-0.251	0.002
	0.159	0.101	0.314	0.018
	-0.247	-0.953	-0.800	0.141

**Significantly different from 0.00 at .05 level.

Appendix D

RESULTS OF ESTIMATES FROM THE COMPOSITE MODEL ANALYSIS

This appendix presents the coefficient estimates for the determinants of the individual models for the composite model analysis. The results of the regional and national level estimates are presented first, followed by the coefficient estimates for the levels of commodities.

Table D.1: Coefficient Estimates of the Interdependence and Dependency Model Equations at Regional and National Level

	CA	ER	GNP	UEP
	b_{i1}	b_{i2}	b_{i3}	b_{i4}
	Stand. Error	Stand. Error	Stand. Error	Stand. Error
	t-ratio	t-ratio	t-ratio	t-ratio
NICs	-0.208*	0.002	-0.056	-0.139
	0.120	0.053	0.198	0.342
	-1.734	0.045	-0.285	-0.407
SIG	-0.004	-0.005	0.026	0.028
	0.005	0.005	0.020	0.038
	-0.666	-1.055	1.299	0.723
KOR	-0.014	-0.016	-0.046	-0.095
	0.031	0.018	0.095	0.173
	-0.459	-0.886	-0.482	-0.547
HK	-0.007	-0.016	-0.046	-0.095
	0.031	0.018	0.095	0.173
	-0.459	-0.886	-0.482	-0.547
TAW	-0.040	0.016	0.088	0.112
	0.035	0.082	0.093	0.115
	-1.138	0.191	0.953	0.974

*Significantly different from 0.00 at .10 level.

Table D.2: Coefficient Estimates of the Mercantilist Model Equations at
Regional and National Level*

	TD1	CF	GE	USTA
	b_{i5}	b_{i6}	b_{i7}	b_{i8}
	Stand. Error	Stand. Error	Stand. Error	Stand. Error
	t-ratio	t-ratio	t-ratio	t-ratio
NICs	0.003	-0.042	0.086	0.005
	0.003	0.024	0.097	0.004
	0.984	-1.767	0.889	1.166
SIG	0.001	-0.000	-0.000	-0.000
	0.000	0.001	0.007	0.001
	2.582	-0.091	-0.015	-0.431
KOR	0.000	-0.007	0.028	0.000
	0.001	0.008	0.029	0.000
	0.305	-0.861	0.982	1.027
HK	0.000	-0.006	-0.047	0.012
	0.001	0.005	0.034	0.010
	0.192	-1.146	-1.372	1.293
TAW	0.001	-0.005	-0.015	-0.000
	0.001	0.010	0.022	0.001
	1.287	-0.487	-0.704	-0.224

* All coefficients not significantly different from 0.00 at .05 level.

Table D.3: Coefficent Estimates of the Interdependence and Dependency
Model Equations at Commodity Level for NICs

NICs	CA	ER	GNP	UEP
	b_{i1}	b_{i2}	b_{i3}	b_{i4}
	Stand. Error	Stand. Error	Stand. Error	Stand. Error
	t-ratio	t-ratio	t-ratio	t-ratio
L1	0.001	0.004	0.037	0.108
	0.007	0.013	0.053	0.101
	0.146	0.275	0.699	1.067
L2	-0.039*	0.088*	-0.290	-0.554***
	0.020	0.043	0.101	0.219
	-1.890	2.042	-2.884	-2.527
L3	-0.069	0.028	-0.107	-0.358
	0.051	0.049	0.202	0.342
	-1.352	0.563	-0.531	-1.047
L4	0.068	-0.017	0.139	1.795
	0.158	0.274	0.910	2.039
	0.428	-0.062	0.153	-1.047
L5	0.052	-0.152	0.262	1.241
	0.086	0.131	0.630	1.226
	0.609	-1.165	0.415	1.013
L6	-0.119	-0.163	-0.251	-0.168
	0.073	0.078	0.269	0.476
	-1.634	-2.091	-0.931	-0.352

*Significantly different from 0.00 at .10 level.
**Significantly different from 0.00 at .05 level.
***Significantly different from 0.00 at .01 level.

Table D.4: Coefficient Estimates of the Mercantilist Model Equations at
Commodity Level for NICs

NICs	TD1 b_{i5} Stand. Error t-ratio	CF b_{i6} Stand. Error t-ratio	GE b_{i7} Stand. Error t-ratio	USTA b_{i8} Stand. Error t-ratio
L1	-0.001	-0.010	0.011	0.000
	0.005	0.006	0.024	0.001
	-0.238	-1.730	0.447	0.234
L2	0.113	-0.011	-0.128	0.012***
	0.080	0.011	0.052	0.004
	1.401	-0.993	-2.445	3.125
L3	0.016	0.010	0.149	-0.000
	0.025	0.021	0.100	0.003
	0.666	0.470	1.495	-0.100
L4	-0.004	-0.086	-0.295	0.022
	0.017	0.092	0.432	0.024
	-0.258	-0.939	-0.683	0.950
L5	0.057	-0.036	-0.088	-0.002
	-0.258	-0.939	-0.683	0.950
	0.608	-0.592	-0.341	-0.104
L6	0.041	-0.045	0.034	-0.015
	0.032	0.027	0.121	0.007
	1.278	-1.688	0.281	-2.050

*** Significantly different from 0.00 at .01 level.

Table D.5: Coefficient Estimates of the Interdependence and Dependency
Model Equations at the Commodity Level for Singapore

	CA	ER	GNP	UEP
	b_{i1}	b_{i2}	b_{i3}	b_{i4}
SIG	Stand. Error	Stand. Error	Stand. Error	Stand. Error
	t-ratio	t-ratio	t-ratio	t-ratio
L1	0.104	0.228	0.469	3.498
	0.097	0.193	0.704	1.421
	1.070	1.183	0.666	2.462
L2	-0.265	0.037	0.466	-7.674**
	0.265	0.468	1.852	3.427
	-1.000	0.472	-2.358	-2.239
L3	0.038	0.037	0.466	0.318
	0.025	0.089	0.311	0.621
	1.521	0.414	1.497	0.511
L4	0.090	-0.270	-0.036	0.787
	0.251	0.301	1.224	2.284
	0.358	-0.899	-0.030	-0.345
L5	0.005	-0.143	-0.029	-0.238
	0.059	0.095	0.330	0.654
	0.087	-1.515	-0.088	-0.364
L6	-0.266	0.155	3.182*	3.388
	0.565	0.458	1.726	3.826
	-0.471	0.338	1.843	0.886

*Significantly different from 0.00 at .10 level.
**Significantly different from 0.00 at .05 level.

Table D.6: Coefficient Estimates of the Mercantilist Model Equations at
the Commodity Level for Singapore

SIG	TD1	CF	GE	USTA
	b_{i5}	b_{i6}	b_{i7}	b_{i8}
	Stand. Error	Stand. Error	Stand. Error	Stand. Error
	t-ratio	t-ratio	t-ratio	t-ratio
L1	-0.098	-0.166	-0.661	-0.013
	0.080	0.045	0.244	0.028
	-1.220	-3.717	-2.712	-0.456
L2	-0.805	-0.131	-0.312	0.006
	1.317	0.144	0.596	0.087
	-0.611	-0.908	-0.522	0.071
L3	-0.087	0.058***	0.004	-0.009
	0.055	0.019	0.112	0.012
	-1.537	3.028	0.003	-0.797
L4	0.031	-0.058	0.083	0.029
	0.031	0.070	0.463	0.047
	0.999	-0.829	0.178	0.625
L5	-0.006	0.002	0.187	0.006
	0.055	0.021	0.123	0.014
	-0.	0.075	1.512	0.448
L6	0.174	0.310**	.0631	0.005
	0.213	0.125	0.651	0.068
	0.818	2.483	0.969	0.071

** Significantly different from 0.00 at .05 level.
***Significantly different from 0.00 at .01 level.

Table D.7: Coefficient Estimates of the Interdependence and Dependency
Model Equations at the Commodity Level for Korea

KOR	CA	ER	GNP	UEP
	b_{i1}	b_{i2}	b_{i3}	b_{i4}
	Stand. Error	Stand. Error	Stand. Error	Stand. Error
	t-ratio	t-ratio	t-ratio	t-ratio
L1	0.003	-0.203	-0.500	-0.636
	0.055	0.075	0.278	0.557
	0.061	-2.710	-1.802	-1.143
L2	0.001	0.005	0.054	0.124
	0.012	0.013	0.087	0.162
	0.075	0.407	0.619	0.767
L3	-0.082	-0.006	-0.100	-0.234
	0.116	0.099	0.466	0.844
	-0.711	-0.062	-0.214	-0.277
L4	-1.413**	-0.721	-20.23	-2.682
	0.676	0.475	2.113	3.707
	-2.091	-1.516	-0.957	-0.724
L5	-0.024	0.058	0.467*	0.645
	0.032	0.048	0.263	0.469
	-0.744	1.212	1.774	1.374
L6	-0.500	-0.188	-0.194	-0.313
	0.341	0.375	1.729	3.092
	-1.469	-0.502	-0.112	-0.101

*Significantly different from 0.00 at .10 level.
**Significantly different from 0.00 at .05 level.

Table D.8: Coefficient Estimates of the Mercantilist Model Equations at
Commodity Level for Korea

KOR	TD1 b_{i5} Stand. Error t-ratio	CF b_{i6} Stand. Error t-ratio	GE b_{i7} Stand. Error t-ratio	USTA b_{i8} Stand. Error t-ratio
L1	0.081	0.000	0.269**	-0.001
	0.041	0.028	0.127	0.002
	1.969	0.001	2.115	-0.449
L2	0.014	0.004	-0.016	0.000
	0.023	0.006	0.015	0.000
	0.608	.0642	-1.051	1.071
L3	0.011	-0.020	-0.009	-0.001
	0.086	0.047	0.169	0.003
	0.130	-0.421	-0.051	-0.430
L4	0.018	-0.224	-0.273	0.003
	0.043	0.201	0.754	0.013
	0.412	-1.110	-0.361	0.242
L5	-0.030	0.031	0.060	0.000
	0.038	0.020	0.079	0.002
	-0.785	1.536	0.754	0.044
L6	0.189	0.133	-0.147	-0.006
	0.186	0.166	0.738	0.010
	1.015	0.802	-0.199	-0.543

**Significantly different from 0.00 at .05 level.

Table D.9: Coefficient Estimates of the Interdependence and Dependency
Model Equations at Commodity Level for Hong Kong

HK	CA	ER	GNP	UEP
	b_{i1}	b_{i2}	b_{i3}	b_{i4}
	Stand. Error	Stand. Error	Stand. Error	Stand. Error
	t-ratio	t-ratio	t-ratio	t-ratio
L1	0.030	0.004	0.012	0.004
	0.009	0.007	0.030	0.054
	3.402	0.549	.0399	0.074
L2	-0.006***	-0.002	-0.005	-0.025
	0.002	0.001	0.008	0.016
	-2.688	-1.214	-0.575	-1.548
L3	-0.041	-0.025	-0.221	-1.058**
	0.064	0.048	0.246	0.485
	-0.645	-0.533	-0.899	-2.180
L4	-0.047	0.032	-0.221	-1.058**
	0.251	0.142	0.967	1.770
	0.185	-0.225	0.650	1.192
L5	-0.126	-0.006	-0.017	-0.658
	0.133	0.074	0.693	1.282
	-0.948	-0.080	-0.025	-0.513
L6	0.298	0.021	-1.029	-2.665
	0.344	0.189	1.075	2.243
	0.868	0.111	-0.958	-1.188

**Significantly different from 0.00 at .05 level.
***Significantly different from 0.00 at .01 level.

Table D.10: Coefficient Estimates of the Mercantilist Model Equations at
Commodity Level for Hong Kong*

HK	TD1 b_{i5} Stand. Error t-ratio	CF b_{i6} Stand. Error t-ratio	GE b_{i7} Stand. Error t-ratio	USTA b_{i8} Stand. Error t-ratio
L1	-0.004	0.005	-0.009	-0.001
	0.004	0.003	0.019	0.005
	-0.925	1.572	-0.452	-0.165
L2	0.010	-0.001	-0.014	0.004
	0.005	0.001	0.007	0.002
	1.902	-1.557	-2.047	1.925
L3	0.110	0.021	0.032	0.039
	0.046	0.019	0.165	0.041
	2.394	1.077	0.194	0.942
L4	-0.009	-0.069	-0.420	0.089
	0.029	0.075	0.775	0.223
	-0.307	-0.928	-0.542	0.398
L5	0.004	0.055	0.394	-0.068
	0.132	0.040	0.452	0.100
	0.032	1.376	0.873	-0.688
L6	0.235	-0.025	0.153	0.209
	0.207	0.112	0.789	0.247
	1.136	-0.223	-0.194	0.845

*All coefficients not significantly different from 0.00 at .05 level.

Table D.11: Coefficient Estimates of the Interdependence and
  Dependency Model Equations at Commodity Level for
  Taiwan*

TAW	CA b_{i1} Stand. Error t-ratio	ER b_{i2} Stand. Error t-ratio	GNP b_{i3} Stand. Error t-ratio	UEP b_{i4} Stand. Error t-ratio
L1	0.013	-0.844	-0.734	0.981
	0.221	0.779	0.961	1.224
	0.058	-1.084	-0.764	0.802
L2	-0.162	0.020	0.002	-0.535
	0.110	0.392	0.441	0.632
	-1.473	0.052	0.005	-0.848
L3	0.066	-0.086	0.030	0.223
	0.062	0.182	0.218	0.256
	1.072	-0.473	0.138	0.873
L4	-0.313	0.150	0.051	-0.072
	0.314	1.218	1.324	1.956
	-0.996	0.123	0.039	-0.037
L5	-0.092	-0.797	-0.681	-0.204
	0.121	0.552	0.650	0.854
	-0.762	-1.444	-1.048	-0.238
L6	-0.607	1.504	1.290	-2.985
	0.486	1.359	1.450	2.126
	-1.248	1.107	0.889	-1.404

*All coefficients not significanlty different from 0.00 at .05 level.

Table D.12: Coefficient Estimates of the Mercantilist Model Equations at
Commodity Level for Taiwan*

TAW	TD1	CF	GE	USTA
	b_{i5}	b_{i6}	b_{i7}	b_{i8}
	Stand. Error	Stand. Error	Stand. Error	Stand. Error
	t-ratio	t-ratio	t-ratio	t-ratio
L1	0.087	-0.145	-0.155	-0.004
	0.097	0.108	0.209	0.012
	0.897	-1.338	-0.740	-0.350
L2	-0.368	0.061	0.099	0.001
	0.157	0.050	0.105	0.005
	-2.341	1.222	0.942	0.177
L3	0.025	-0.023	0.058	0.002
	0.028	0.026	0.074	0.003
	0.903	-0.921	0.784	0.855
L4	-0.017	0.080	0.226	-0.007
	0.028	0.170	0.310	0.020
	-0.626	0.469	0.727	-0.367
L5	0.039	-0.082	-0.086	-0.002
	0.063	0.073	0.125	0.007
	0.609	-1.130	-0.686	-0.297
L6	0.057	0.243	0.046	-0.003
	0.241	0.201	0.332	0.030
	0.236	1.212	0.138	-0.092

*All Coefficients not significantly different from 0.00 at .05 level.

Appendix E

UNITED STATES BUDGET AND TRADE DEFICITS

This appendix provides the magnitude and trend of the United States budget and trade deficits.

Table E.1: U.S. Budget and Trade Deficits, 1967-1987 ($ millions)

Year	Budget Deficit	Trade Deficit	U.S. Trade Balance with:				
			SIG	KOR	HK	TAW	JAP
1967	-8700	4714	50	297	-243	167	-304
1968	-25200	1299	73	312	-333	117	-1107
1969	3200	1963	97	408	-451	5	-1398
1970	-2800	3272	159	273	-538	-22	-1223
1971	-23000	-1465	179	219	-567	-307	-3206
1972	-23200	-5784	120	27	-760	-665	-4101
1973	-14300	1863	224	272	-704	-605	-1363
1974	-3500	-2466	435	86	-755	-680	-1776
1975	-43600	10690	460	320	-765	-287	-1862
1976	-73700	-5680	270	-389	-1296	-1354	-5360
1977	-53600	-26459	289	-512	-1602	-1873	-8021
1978	-59200	-28315	394	-586	-1849	-2828	-11573
1979	-40200	-24525	863	-143	-1923	-2630	-8664
1980	-73800	-24088	1112	538	-2053	-2517	-9924
1981	-78900	-27600	889	-111	-2793	-3744	-18081
1982	-127900	-31677	1019	-108	-3087	-4526	-18965
1983	-207800	-57510	891	-1223	-3830	-6537	-21665
1984	-185300	-107838	-304	-3370	-5204	-9765	-36796
1985	-212300	-148493	-937	-4756	-6208	-13061	-49749
1986	-221200	-169789	-1504	-7142	-6443	-15727	-58575
1987	-150400	-171230	-2342	-9892	-6507	-18994	-59825

Source: U.S. Department of Commerce, *U.S. Foreign Trade Highlights* and *Statistical Abstract of the Untied States.*

Table E.2: The NICs and Japan' Trade Surplus as Percent of U.S. Trade
Deficit, 1967-87*

Year	SIG	KOR	HK	TAW	NIC	JAP
1967	NA	NA	NA	NA	NA	NA
1968	NA	NA	NA	NA	NA	NA
1969	NA	NA	NA	NA	NA	NA
1970	NA	NA	NA	NA	NA	NA
1971	NA	NA	38.70%	20.96%	32.49%	218.84%
1972	NA	NA	13.14%	11.50%	22.10%	70.90%
1973	NA	NA	NA	NA	NA	NA
1974	NA	NA	30.62%	27.58%	37.06%	72.02%
1975	NA	NA	NA	NA	NA	NA
1976	NA	6.85%	22.82%	23.84%	48.75%	94.37%
1977	NA	1.94%	6.05%	7.08%	13.98%	30.31%
1978	NA	2.07%	6.53%	9.99%	17.20%	40.87%
1979	NA	0.58%	7.84%	10.72%	15.63%	35.33%
1980	NA	NA	8.52%	10.45%	12.12%	41.20%
1982	NA	0.34%	9.75%	14.29%	21.16%	59.87%
1983	NA	2.13%	6.66%	11.37%	18.60%	37.67%
1984	0.28%	3.13%	4.83%	9.06%	17.29%	34.12%
1985	0.63%	3.20%	4.18%	8.80%	16.81%	33.50%
1986	0.89%	4.21%	3.79%	9.26%	18.15%	34.50%
1987	1.37%	5.78%	3.80%	11.09%	22.04%	34.94%

*NA is assigned when the United States has trade surplus or when
exporting countries do not have trade surplus with the U.S.

Bibliography

Balaam, David N., and Michael Veseth. ed. *Readings in International Political Economy*. Upper Saddle River, NJ: Prentice Hall, 1996.

Balassa, Bela, and John Williamson. *Adjusting to Success: Balance of Payments Policy in the East Asian NICs*. Washington, DC: Institute for International Economics, 1987.

Baldwin, Robert E. *The Political Economy of U.S. Import Policy*. Cambridge, MA: MIT Press, 1985.

Baran, Paul. "On the Political Economy of Backwardness." *The Manchester School* January (1952): 66-84.

Bauer, Raymond A., I. Pool, and L. Dexter. *American Business and Public Policy: The Politics of Foreign Trade*. New York: Atherson Press, 1964.

Bergsten, C. Fred. *America in the World Economy: A Strategy for the 1990s*. Washington, DC: Institute for International Economics, 1988a.

------. "US International Macroeconomic Policy." In *Economic Relations between the United States and Korea: Conflict or Cooperation*. Ed. Thomas Bayard and Soo-Gil Young, Washington, DC: Institute for International Economics, 1988b.

Bergsten, C. Fred, and William R. Cline. *The United States--Japan Economic Problem*. Washington, DC: Institute for International Economics, 1987.

Bergsten, C. Fred, and John Williamson. "Exchange Rates and Trade Policy." In *Trade Policy in the 1980s*. Ed. William Cline. Washington, DC: Institute for International Economics, 1983.

Bhagwati, Jagdish N. ed. *Import Competition and Response*. Chicago: University of Chicago Press, 1982.

------. *The World Trading System at Risk*. Princeton: Princeton University Press, 1991.

Borthwick, Mark. *Pacific Century: The Emergence of Modern Pacific Asia*. Boulder, CO: Westview Press, 1992.

Brander, James A. "Rationales for Strategic Trade and Industrial Policy." In *Strategic Trade Policy and New International Economics*. Ed. Paul Krugman. Cambridge, MA: MIT Press, 1986.

Brewer, Anthony. *Marxist Theories of Imperialism: A Critical Survey*. London: Routledege & Kegan Paul, 1980.

Caporaso, James A. "Industrialization in the Periphery." *International Studies Quarterly* 25 (1981): 347-384.

Cardoso, Fernando H. "Associated-Dependent Development." In *Authoritarian Brazil*. Ed. Alfred Stephan. New Haven: Yale University Press, 1973.

Chatfield, C. *The Analysis of Time Series: An Introduction*. 3rd ed. London: Chapman and Hall, 1985.

Clark, Cal, and Steven Chan. ed. *The Evolving Pacific Basin in the Global Political Economy*. Boulder, CO: Lynne Rienner, 1992.

Cline, William R. *Reciprocity: A New Approach to World Trade Policy?*. Washington, DC: Institute for International Economics, 1982.

------. *International Debt and the Stability of the World Economy*. Washington, DC: Institute for International Economics, 1983.

------. *Exports of Manufactured From Developing Countries*. Washington, DC: Brookings Institution, 1984.

------. *The Future of World Trade in Textiles and Apparel*. Washington, DC: Institute for International Economics, 1987.

Cooper, Richard. *The Economics of Interdependence*. New York: McGraw Hill, 1968.

------. *Economic Policy in an Interdependent World: Essays in World Economics*. Cambridge, MA: MIT Press, 1986.

Crane, George T., and Abla Amawi. ed. *The Theoretical Evolution of International Political Economy*. New York: Oxford University Press, 1991.

Cumings, Bruce. "The Origins and Development of Northeast Asian Political Economy: Industrial Sectors, Product Cycles, and Political Consequences." *International Organization* 38 (1984): 1-40.

Cuomo Commission Report. Cuomo Commission on Trade and Competitiveness. New York: Touchstone Book, 1988.

Curtis, Gerald L. ed. *The United States, Japan and Asia: Challenges for U.S. Policy*. New York: W.W. Norton, 1994.

Destler, I.M. *American Trade Politics: System Under Stress*. Washington, DC: Institute for International Economics, 1986.

Destler, I.M., and John Odell. *Anti-Protection: Changing Forces in United States Trade Politics*. Washington, DC: Institute for International Economics, 1987.

Dickson, Bruce, and Harry Harding. *Economic Relations in the Asian Pacific Region*. Washington, DC: Brookings Institution, 1987.

Dornbusch, Rudiger, and Jefferey A. Frankel "Macroeconomics and Protection." In *U.S. Trade Policies in a Changing World Economy*. Ed. Robert H. Stern. Cambridge, MA: MIT Press, 1987.

Dos Santos, Theotonio "Historical Perspectives on Political Economy." In *International Politics*. Ed. Robert Art and Robert Jervis. Boston: Little Brown and Company, 1985.

Carr, E. H. *The Twenty Years' Crisis, 1919-1939*. London: St. Martin's Press, 1939.

Chase-Dunn, Christopher K. "Interstate System and Capitalist World Economy: One Logic or Two?" *International Studies Quarterly* 25 (1981): 19-42.

Engle, Robert F. "Specification of the Disturbances for Efficient Estimation." *Econometrica* 41 (1974): 225-38.

Evans, Peter. *Dependent Development: The Alliance of Multinational, State and Local Capital in Brazil*. Princeton: Princeton University Press, 1979.

Feldstein, Martin. ed. *The American Economy in Transition*. Chicago: University of Chicago Press, 1980.

------. ed. *International Economic Cooperation*. Chicago: University of Chicago Press, 1988.

Firebaugh, Glenn, and Bradley P. Bullock. "Level of Processing of Exports: Estimates for Developing Nations." *International Studies Quarterly* 30 (1986): 333-350.

Finlay, Ronald. "Factor Proportions and Comparative Advantage in the Long Run." In *International Trade: Select Readings*. Ed. Jagdish N. Bhagwati. Cambridege, MA: MIT Press, 1981.

Frank, Andre Gunder. "The Development of Underdevelopment." *Monthly Review* 18 (1966) : 17-31.

Frey, Bruno S. *International Political Economics*. New York: Basil Blackwell, 1984.

Frieden, Jeffry A., and David A. Lake. ed. *International Political Economy: Perspectives on Global Power and Wealth*. 3rd ed. New York: St. Martin's Press, 1995.

Gereffi, Gary, and Donald L. Wyman. ed. *Manufacturing Miracles: Paths of Industrialization in Latin America and East Asia*. Princeton:

Princeton University Press, 1990.

Gilpin, Robert. "Three Models of the Future." In *World Politics and International Economics*. Ed. C. Fred Bergsten and Lawrence Krause. Washington, D.C.: Brookings Institution, 1975b.

------. *US Power and the Multinational Corporation: The Political Economy of Foreign Direct Investment*. New York: Basic Books, 1975a.

------. "The Nature of Political Economy." In *International Politics*. Ed. Robert Art and Robert Jervis. Boston: Little, Brown and Company, 1985.

Glitman, Russell. "Korean Firms Chalk Up Surprising Sales Success In the U.S. Micro Market." *PC Week* 9 September 1986, 181-83.

Goldstein, Judith. "The Political Economy of Trade." *American Political Science Review* 80 (1986): 161-184

Graham, Norman A. *The Impact of Foreign Industrial Practices on the U.S. Computer Industry*. Glastonbury, CT: The Futures Group, 1985.

Haggard, Stephan. "The Newly Industrializing Countries in the International System." *World Politics* 38 (1986) : 343-70.

------. *Pathways from the Periphery: The Politics of Growth in the Newly Industrializing Countries*. Itahca, NY: Cornell University Press, 1990.

Haggard, Stephan, and Robert R. Kaufman. ed. *The Politics of Economic Adjustment*. Princeton: Princeton University Press, 1992.

Haggard, Stephan, and Chung In Moon. "The South Korean State in the International Economy: Liberal, Dependent, or Mercantile?" In *The Antinomies of Interdependence*. Ed. John Ruggie. New York: Columbia University Press, 1983.

Hanushek, Eric A., and John E. Jackson. *Statistical Methods for Social Scientists*. New York: Academic Press, 1977.

Harris, Niegel. *The End of the Third World: Newly Industrializing Countries and the Decline of an Ideology*. New York: Penguin Books, 1986.

Hirschman, Albert. *National Power and the Structure of Foreign Trade*. Berkeley: University of California Press, 1980.

Huntington, Samuel P. "Transnational Organization in World Politics." *World Politics* 25 (1973): 333-368.

Jackman, Robert W. "Dependence on Foreign Investment and Economic Growth in the Third World." *World Politics* 34 (1982): 175-96.

Johnston, J. *Econometric Methods*. 3rd ed. New York: McGraw-Hill, 1984.

Jones, Ronald W. "The Structure of Simple General Equilibrium Model." In *International Trade: Select Readings*. Ed. Jagdish N. Bhagwati. Cambridege, MA: MIT Press, 1981.

Judge, George, Griffiths, W.E., Hill, R. Carter, H. Lutkepohl, and T.C.Lee. The Theory and Practice of Econometrics. 2nd ed. New York: John Wiley and Sons, 1985.

Kennedy, Peter. *A Guide to Econometrics*. 2nd ed. Cambridege, MA: MIT Press, 1985.

Keohane, Robert O. *After Hegemony: Cooperation and Discord in the World Political Economy*. Princeton: Princeton University Press, 1984.

Keohane, Robert O., and Joseph S. Nye. *Power and Interdependence: World Politics in Transition*. 2nd ed. Boston: Little, Brown and Company, 1989.

Kindleberger, Charles P., and Peter H. Lindert. *International Economics*. 6th ed. Homewood, IL: Richard Irwin, Inc, 1978.

Kmenta, Jan. *Elements of Econometrics*. 2nd ed. New York: Macmillan Publishing, 1986.

Knorr, Klaus. *The Power of Nations: The Political Economy of International Relations*. New York: Basic Books, 1975.

Krasner, Stephen D. "State Power and the Structure of International Trade." *World Politics* 28 (1976): 317-348.

------. *Defending the National Interest: Raw Materials Investment and U.S. Foreign Policy*. Princeton: Princeton University Press, 1978.

------. *Structural Conflict: The Third World Against Global Liberalism*. Berkeley: University of Calif. Press , 1985.

Krause, Lawrence B. "The Developing Countries and American Interests." In *The Pacific Basin: New Challenges for the United States*. Ed. James Morley. New York: Academy of Political Science, 1986.

Kurth, James R. "The Political Consequences of the Product Cycle." *International Organization* 33 (1979): 1-34.

Krugman, Paul R. "Introduction: New Thinking about Trade Policy." In *Strategic Trade Policy and New International Economics*. Paul Krugman. Cambridge, MA: MIT Press, 1986.

Lairson, Thomas D., and David Skidmore. *International Political Economy: The Struggle for Power and Wealth*. Fort Worth, TX: Hold, Rinehat and Winston, 1993.

Lawrence, Robert Z., and Charles L. Schultze. ed. *An American Trade Strategy: Options for the 1990s*. Washington, D.C. : Brookings

Institution, 1990.

Leamer, Edward E. *Sources of International Comparative Advantage: Theory and Evidence.* Cambridge, MA: MIT Press, 1984.

Lehman, Jean-Pierre. "Dictatorship and Development in Pacific Asia: Wider Implication." *International Affairs* 61 (1985): 591-606.

Linder, Staffan B. *The Pacific Century: Economic and Political Consequences of Asian Pacific Dynamism.* Stanford: Stanford University Press, 1986.

Lundestad, Geir. *East, West, North, South: Major Developments in International Politics 1945-1986.* Oslo: Norwegian University Press, 1986.

------. *The American "Empire."* London: Oxford University Press, 1990.

Morse, Edward L. "Interdependence in World Affairs." In *World Politics.* James Rosneau, et al. New York: Free Press, 1976.

Nam, Chong-Hyun. "Export-Promoting Subsidies, Countervailing Threats, and the General Agreement on Tariffs and Trade." *The World Bank Economic Review.* 1 (1987): 727-43.

Nau, Henry R. *The Myth of America's Decline.* New York: Oxford University Press, 1990.

Nivola, Pietro S. "The New Protectionism: U.S. Trade Policy in Historical Perspective." *Political Science Quarterly* 101 (1986): 577-600.

North Douglass C. *Institutions, Institutional Change and Economic Performance.* New York: Cambridge University Press, 1990.

Odell, John S. "Latin American Trade Negotiation with the United States." *International Organizations* 34 (1980): 207-28.

------. "The Outcomes of International Trade Conflicts: The US and South Korea, 1960-1981." *International Studies Quarterly* 29 (1985): 263-286.

Odell, John S., and Thomas D. Willett. ed. *International Trade Policies.* Ann Arbor: University of Michigan Press, 1993.

Ohlin, Bertil. *Interregional and International Trade.* revised ed. Cambridge, MA: Harvard University Press, 1967.

Okita, Saburo. "Pacific Development and Its Implications for the World Economy." In *The Pacific Basin: New Challenges for the United States.* Ed. James Morley. New York: Academy of Political Science, 1986.

Paik, Won K. "Dependent Development and International Trading System: A Poststructural Analysis." *The Korean Journal of International Studies* 19 (1987): 517-36.

------. "Causes of Import Penetration from the Pacific Basin Newly

Industrializing Countries into the United States." *Journal of Southeast Asian Studies* 22 (1991): 361-378.

Paik, Won K., and Russell Mardon. "Industrial Policies and Economic Performance of South Korea." *Pacific Focus* VI (1991): 59-76.

------. "The State, Foreign Investment and Sustaining Industrial Growth in South Korea and Thailand." In. *The Evolving Pacific Basin in the Global Political Economy.* Ed. Cal Clark and Steven Chan. Boulder, CO: Lynne Rienner, 1992.

Patrick, Hugh."The Burgeoning American Economic Stake in the Pacific Basin." In *The Pacific Basin: New Challenges for the United States.* Ed. James Morley. New York: Academy of Political Science, 1986.

Pirages, Dennis. *Global Technopolitics: The International Politics of Technology and Resources.* Pacific Grove, CA: Brooks/Cole Publishing, 1989.

Rhee, Hak-Yong "Protection Structures of the Developing Countries in Pacific Asia" *Asia-Yungu* 27 (1984): 419-40.

Ricardo, David. *The Principles of Political Economy and Taxation.* London: Dent and Sons, 1973.

Rogowski, Ronald. *Commerce and Coalitions: How Trade affects Domestic Political Alignments.* Princeton, NJ: Princeton University Press, 1989.

Rosecrane, Richard. *America's Economic Resurgence: A Bold New Strategy.* New York: Harpers & Row, 1990.

Sachs, Jeffrey D. ed. *Developing Country Debt and the World Economy.* Chicago: University of Chicago Press, 1989.

Schattschneider, E. E. *Politics, Pressures and Tariff.* New York: Prentice Hall, 1935.

Schott, Jeffrey J. "US Trade Policy: Implications for US-Korea Relations." In *Economic Relations between the United States and Korea: Conflict or Cooperation.* Ed. Thomas Bayard and Soo-Gil Young. Washington, DC: Institute for International Economics, 1988.

Schwartz, Herman M. *States Versus Markets: History, Geography, and the Development of International Political Economy.* New York: St. Martin's Press, 1994.

Smith, Adam. *An Inquiry into the Nature and Causes of The Wealth of Nations.* Chicago: University of Chicago Press, 1976.

Smith, Tony. *The Patterns of Imperialism.* Cambridge, London: Cambridge University Press, 1981.

Sneider, Richard. "United States Security Interest." In *The Pacific Basin:*

New Challenges for the United States. Ed. James Morley. New York: Academy of Political Science, 1986.

Spero, Joan Edelman. *The Politics of International Economic Relations.* 3rd ed. New York: St. Martin's Press, 1985.

Stiles, Kendall W., and Tsuneo Akaha. ed. *International Political Economy: A Reader.* New York: HarperCollins, 1991.

Strange, Susan. "The management of Surplus Capacity: Or How Does Theory Stand Up to Protectionism 1970s Style?" *International Organization* 33 (1979): 303-333.

------. "Protectionism and World Politics." *International Organization* 39 (1985) : 233-259.

Stokes, Bruce. "A Thorny Agenda Facing Eximbank." *National Journal* 45 (1988): 2800-01.

Sylvan, David J. "The Newest Mercantilism." *International Organization* 35 (1981): 375-393.

United Nations. *Industrial Statistics Yearbook. Vol.1: General Industrial Statistics.* New York: United Nations, 1967-85.

------. *Yearbook of National Account Statistics.* New York: United Nations, 1970-1985.

U.S. Department of Commerce. *U.S. General Imports: World Area by Commodity Groupings (FT 155).* Washington, D.C.: U.S. Government Printing Office, 1967-1985.

------. *U.S. Foreign Trade Highlights.* Washington, D.C.: U.S. Government Printing Office, 1987.

------. *U.S. Merchandise Trade Position.* Washington, D.C.: U.S. Government Printing Office, 1988.

U.S. Bureau of Census. *Statistical Abstract of the United States.* Washington, D.C.: U.S. Government Printing Office, 1967-1987.

U.S. International Trade Commission. *Annual Report.* Washington, D.C.: International Trade Commission, 1967-1988.

Vernon, Raymon. *Sovereignty At Bay: The Multinational Spread of US Enterprises.* New York: Basic Books, 1971.

------. "International Trade Policy in the 1980s." *International Studies Quarterly* 26 (1982) : 483-510.

Vernon, Raymond, and Debora Spar. *Beyond Globalism: Remaking American Foreign Economic Policy.* New York: Free Press, 1989.

Viner, Jacob. "Power Versus Plenty as Objectives of Foreign Policy in the Seventeenth and Eighteenth Centuries." *World Politics* 1 (1948): 1-29.

Walleri, R. Dan. "The Political Economy Literature of North-South Relations." *International Studies Quarterly* 22 (1978) : 587-624.

Wallerstein, Immanuel. *The Modern World System.* New York: Academic Press, 1974.

------. *The Capitalist World Economy.* London: Cambridge University Press, 1979.

Walters, Robert S., and David H. Blake. *The Politics of Global Economic Relations.* 4th ed. Englewwod Cliffs, NJ: Prentice-Hall, 1992.

Waltz, Kenneth. *Man, the State, and War: A Theoretical Analysis.* New York: Columbia University Press, 1954.

Wilber, Charles K. ed. *The Political Economy of Development and Underdevelopment.* New York: Random House, 1988.

World Bank. *Korea: Managing the Industrial Transition.* Washington, DC: The World Bank, 1988.

Yoffi, David B. *Power and Protectionism.* Princeton: Princeton University Press, 1983.

Index